Bernard Salt is widely regarded as Australia's leading social commentator, having appeared regularly on radio and television programs for more than twenty years. He is a twice-weekly columnist with *The Australian* newspaper, a business advisor as a KPMG Partner and a corporate speaker at the highest level. *Decent Obsessions* is Bernard's fifth book in just over a decade.

DECENT
OBSESSIONS
Why it's okay to sweat
the small stuff

BERNARD SALT

MELBOURNE
UNIVERSITY
PRESS

MELBOURNE UNIVERSITY PRESS
An imprint of Melbourne University Publishing Limited
11–15 Argyle Place South, Carlton, Victoria 3053, Australia
mup-info@unimelb.edu.au
www.mup.com.au

First published 2013
Reprinted 2013
Text © Bernard Salt, 2013
Design and typography © Melbourne University Publishing Limited, 2013

Every attempt has been made to locate the copyright holders for material quoted in this book. Any person or organisation that may have been overlooked or misattributed may contact the publisher.

Cover design by Design by Committee
Typeset by Sonya Murphy
Printed in Australia by McPherson's Printing Group

National Library of Australia Cataloguing-in-Publication entry

Salt, Bernard, 1956–
Decent obsessions/Bernard Salt.

9780522862720 (paperback)
9780522862737 (ebook)
Etiquette.
Courtesy.

Contents

1

Decent Obsessions

WHEN I was a kid growing up in the 1960s in a Housing Commission house in a small country town in Victoria with my parents and five siblings, there wasn't much time, or inclination I must say, for me (or for any kid that I knew) to be considered special. And now almost half a century later I find that nothing has changed. Do you know why? It's because I am white, male, middle-aged and middle-class. I am also heterosexual and able-bodied, have an Anglo-Celtic Christian heritage, live within a family environment and work within 'greedy' corporate Australia. And I have no deep-seated psychological issues. (Please don't smirk.) I am not depressed. I was not abused as a child or as an altar boy. I am the antithesis of special. I am the embodiment of anti-special.

I have nothing to complain about. I wasn't special as a kid and I can in no way be considered special as an adult. In fact I am privileged. I am privileged to work hard and to be taxed accordingly. Apparently. Whenever there are concessions and special deals and off-peak rates being doled out, do you know where I am? I'm at the back of the queue. And that's because I get to pay for everyone else—because I am so privileged and because I have had it so easy.

There is no legitimate reason why anyone should cut me any slack. Not that I want any slack, but it would be nice to know that if ever I did want special consideration there was some stored somewhere for me to, well, be considered special. It is instructive that at this point I feel compelled to place my comments in context. I know there are people with special needs and those who have been, and who still are being, unfairly and unreasonably discriminated against. I understand this; I acknowledge this; I respect this. But what about me? And people like me? There is a case to make about the polite and dutiful middle class. We pay our taxes; we do our best to raise good kids; we work hard; we maintain the family unit as best we can; we don't cause trouble. And what do we get for our efforts? Vilification. Anyone who works for corporate Australia is automatically part of an elite 'who should pay even more tax'. Well here's the thing. I think I work hard and that I don't deserve the opprobrium that comes from those who have not been prepared to put in the same effort. I choose not to live on the edge; I choose to live in the centre. Life is better there. It may be less exciting, but for me and for millions of others we see it as largely a matter of choice. Yes, yes, I know there are those for whom life on the edge is not a choice but a sad reality. Yes, yes, I know there are those who are generationally and systemically caught within welfare traps and who can only dream of a middle-class lifestyle. But is it wrong to suggest that these circumstances should never be an excuse for not doing what you can to improve your lot? I did it. Others can do it too. At some point the hard-working middle class has to stand up and say enough's enough. If so many people are deserving of special attention and special concessions, then, excuse me, but who is doing the work? Who is paying for all this? And there is one group who it might be said have done it toughest. Middle-aged workers who have put in thirty years' hard labour and who have transitioned from battler class to middle class. This lot didn't get the advantages of an idle, middle-class youth. What they got was the opportunity to put in year after year and to be rewarded for their efforts with being derided 'because they're rich'.

In Australia as well as in many other developed nations you too can become well-to-do, even rich, if you work hard enough and consistently enough. Welcome to my world of decent obsessions. In this world people make rational decisions and act fairly and reasonably. They don't impose on others. They act normally, if a tad conservatively, and they don't require the effort or attention of others to live meaningful lives. I get up; I go to work; I pay my bills; I try to be a good parent; I have long-term relationships; and I can engage in balanced small talk with other people without redirecting the conversation back to me, my life and my kids. Experience has taught me this is hard to do for many.

It's not rocket science. Get a job and work at it. Don't spend more money each week than you make. No one owes you anything despite the fact that parents, teachers, employers and Facebook friends have told you that you are special. You are not special. You and I and many others are quite ordinary. You will never be rich or famous or win TattsLotto. No. I'm sorry you won't. Your boss isn't psychotic; your co-workers aren't sociopaths. Sometimes you need to work things through and to persist. That's an odd word, isn't it? *Persist*. It means to continue doing something that might be a tad boring and not very water-cooler-worthy in the eyes of your friends, who always seem to be doing exciting things. Eventually this concept of 'persisting' will deliver you a better quality of life by middle age than the alternative of pursuing every one of life's options. And this includes, for example, the option of blowing it all on 'wonderful life experiences' but then have nothing to show for it by thirty. And when you have nothing to show for it at thirty you will no doubt look around and complain bitterly about all those people who had it easy.

I was married at twenty-two; I had a mortgage at twenty-four; I had children at thirty; I have worked for four employers in thirty years. For many, life is what you make of it; for some there are constraints. My advice to generation Y is to look at the big picture and the long term; my advice to boomers is that what you have in your fifties is probably the sum total of your own efforts. You are not wealthy because you didn't make the right choices or take the right risks or—you're gonna love this one—have the right abilities and insight at the right time in life.

No middle-aged person wants to confront the reality that they made bad choices; they want to believe that the only reason why they aren't on the BRW Rich 200 list is because of some factor beyond their control: they married the wrong person; they didn't get access to university; they were born in the wrong place; they didn't receive adequate support from parents, employers or others. No. The reason why middle-aged boomers aren't on the BRW Rich 200 list is because they more often than not lacked the talent, the application, the courage and the insight to do what was required in their twenties. Tough call that one. Easier to hold onto the dream that you would have made it but for the intervention or the non-intervention of others.

Decent Obsessions is a book of columns written to a consistent theme: that there is a 'them' and an 'us'. We work hard and pay tax and lead normal lives, and this effort goes into supporting the lifestyles of some who pursue, shall we say, edgier existences. We all know people like this. The relative who is constantly broke but who manages to find sufficient funds to flit off to Bali for a holiday 'because they've had a rough trot lately'. The self-obsessed 'friend' who dominates conversation. Those who stay out late, who are self-obsessed, who invariably make silly choices in relationships, in jobs and especially with regard to money. Why should those who manage their lives well and who exercise self-control and discipline be forced to listen to or otherwise engage with those who live beyond their means and efforts? The centre, the comfortable, the safe and the secure are all ruthlessly parodied, and yet it is within these confines that the real drivers of society reside. My Saturday columns with *The Australian* newspaper have provided me with an outlet to vent quietly about the trials and tribulations of the pursuit of a normal life. It is a view of life from the middle of the bell curve. They have struck a chord with many. Welcome to my decent obsessions. This a cry of the heart, a *cri de cœur* from the middle aged and the middle class. We've had enough of your edgy ways. Come back into the fold, behave normally, and don't ever leave the television volume on an odd, let alone a prime number again.

2

Obsession and Insight

NOWHERE is the minutiae of human thought more focused than in the special category of obsession and insight. Obsession, of course, is that which engages us to perhaps an unhealthy degree, whereas insight is more of a revelation, a new way of looking at things. People will happily chat on about their insights; obsessions, on the other hand, are more likely to be secreted in the darker recesses of the mind. Well I say bring them both into the sunlight so that we might better understand the matters that engage, amuse and infuriate us on a daily basis. An obsession can relate to time and the need to control it, or lists and the need to make them, or phones and the urge to check for messages, or the inexplicable preference to settle the television volume on an even number. Insight is a softer, more caring version of obsession: it pretends to be more cerebral but in many respects is just a milder form of obsession. For example, is developing a theory about French men by sitting in a Parisian sidewalk café peering at sockless male ankles an insight or is it an obsession? Or it is something else altogether? Regardless, it's what occupies mind space, and as such it fulfils all that is required to be a decent obsession.

First of all, note that every second counts

To some people, *now* doesn't mean 'now', it means as soon as they can

I WANT to talk about a much-misunderstood concept. I want to talk about time. I have been operating on the assumption that time was the same for everyone. Or at least everyone within the same meridian. Oh, I do so like using the word *meridian* in context in a sentence; it makes me feel so, so—oh I don't know—geographical? And frankly, who wouldn't want to feel a teensy bit geographical? I know I do. Frequently. However, it has taken me a lifetime to realise that time is not as it seems. Time bends. Time shifts. Time shuffles. Time for me is not the same as time for you. Time for me is right here, right now, right this instant. Time for me is an immovable fact.

If I say, 'Is everyone ready to go?' and start walking to the car, then I assume that everyone who heard me and who explicitly or tacitly agreed that they too are ready to go is also walking to the car. But not so. Some people—okay, okay, some people of a gender other than male—dillydally; they shilly-shally; they dawdle; they get waylaid; they find things that need to be done on the way to the car. No. If you give an undertaking to a driver—okay, okay, to a male driver—that you are ready to go, it does not mean opportunistically finding stuff to do along the way. Walking to the car is not a multi-tasking opportunity. The hall table does not need dusting. The front doormat does not need shaking. Junk mail can remain in the letterbox. Yes, really it can. No one is going to steal junk mail. I promise. Can we please go? You don't understand. When men say they need to go, we need to, you know, go. There is a demonic inner-male driving urge that once set in motion is quite unstoppable. You can't toy with the primal male driving urge like that. It's cruel. It's just as well that this discussion is of a general nature and does not refer to any institution, individual or group of individuals, otherwise I might find myself in a bit of trouble this Saturday morning.

Yes, I suppose there is the remote possibility that I might be a tad prescriptive about time. But I don't think so. Let me run this test past you. Do you think it's unreasonable to say to a waiter that you would like a cup of tea, but if he is unable to bring it within five minutes, then to perhaps leave it, as you need to go? Is it fair to place terms, conditions and time frames on the delivery of service by a waiter? I say it's okay as long as the request is politely pitched. Others who are, shall we say, less prescriptive about time say there is a sacred social contract that exists between the waiter and the waited upon: this contract stipulates that the waiter has sovereignty over their time and that to impose conditions and time frames is a threat to that intrinsic sovereignty. I say that the waiter cedes sovereignty over their time, or should so cede such sovereignty, for the duration that they are on duty, and for this reason a time-conditioned request for the delivery of a cup of tea is perfectly acceptable. I have yet to put my time-conditioned tea request to a waiter, but as you can see, I have very much applied my mind to the subject and will be prepared should the need arise.

And now, if you will excuse me, I have to attend a meeting that is due to start at 9 am, and as it is 8.57 am and the meeting room is two minutes' walk from my office, I must leave now. Otherwise I will be late and that would never do.

Car space, the final frontier

Is it possible to lust after a parking space?

SO there I am at 2 pm on a Saturday, prowling the Hawthorn Bunnings car park in Melbourne, looking for a place to park. Some people are lucky in this respect: the ideal parking space will magically materialise before their eyes just when they need it. I'm the opposite. I have to wait and queue and drive around, and when I do see a vacant spot, it's invariably a tight one next to a concrete pillar at the farthest point possible from where I need to go. Do you believe in the concept of PSE, or parking spot envy? Do you ever look at parking spots and think, Why don't I ever happen across a desirable spot such as that: wide, no concrete pillars, next to the store entrance, easy to reverse out of? Sigh. Sometimes these undeniably desirable spaces in the car park are painted, so your tyres squeak when you pull in. I don't know about you, but I quite like a bit of car-park tyre squeak. It makes me feel clean. Come on, admit it, you do, too. It's okay; it's quite natural to feel this way.

Do you know my favourite parking spaces? Come close. I don't want everyone knowing this. There are about six spaces outside the ground-floor car-park entrance to David Jones in the Chadstone Shopping Centre that are quite possibly the most desirable parking places I have seen: wide, under cover, pillarless, painted concrete floor, easy to get in to and out of, next to the entrance. I mean right next to the entrance. One or two steps and you're at the perfume counter. How good is that? I'll have to stop now. I'm coming over all faint. In fact I'm a bit flushed. But of course these car spaces are in such demand that they're always full. Do you think it's odd that a grown man should think—hmmm, shall we say longingly?—about parking spaces? No? Good, neither do I. In fact I would say that such musings are perfectly normal. But let me assure you that one day I intend having one of those parking spaces. Fully and completely. For hours, not minutes. Hours. And why not? After all, someone has to park in those spaces. Why can't it be me?

I have an aunty who says a prayer whenever she needs a space in a car park. And she says it never fails. I suspect that's the reason why people like me—people of marginal and dubious faith—never get the good spots. God is in cahoots with devout aunties and others, giving them the best parking spots. Sinners, on the other hand, are banished to the sheer hell, or at least purgatory, of remote, unpainted, tight spaces near concrete pillars that take ten-point turns to get in to and out of.

However, PSE is but one emotion that surfaces in the relentless hunt for a parking space. The other is repressed rage at being kept waiting by someone who knows you're waiting for their space. Look, Bunnings-car-space-hogging fella, if you get into your car and put your foot on the brake pedal and put gears into reverse so that brake and reversing lights glow in anticipation of some car-moving action, then I expect you to follow through and deliver on your intent, if not your word. In fact I'll be blunt: brake lights on means I expect you to pull out forthwith. Clearly there are car-park teasers who are always promising to vacate a spot but who never deliver. It takes nerve to look someone who is walking to their car in the eye and sum them up as a car-park tease. No, I won't wait for you to leave because you look like a car-park tease. I have more dignity than that. I'll take my chances out in the parking-bay fray rather than invest my time and emotion in waiting in vain for you to get moving. And I hope that when you finally do leave, you will see me luxuriating in one of those well-positioned, amply proportioned, painted-floor, pillarless, under-cover parking spaces that everyone—that's right, everyone—so badly wants.

The first thing to do is make a list

There are those who make lists and those who don't

I WOULD like to talk to you about a very serious issue. A very serious issue indeed. I want to talk to you about a terrible affliction that is, well, afflicting all sorts of people. Not me. I am, fortunately, immune from this disease. Why? Because I have the capacity to operate on a whim, in the moment, without a plan. I am a man without a plan, and a man without a plan is a man who doesn't need a list.

Do you know there are some people who create lists for everything? That's right. The world just does not operate fluidly for these people unless they're writing out and referring to and checking off lists. They suffer from a condition known as compulsive obsessive list-making disorder, or COLD. This is an affliction that can start quite young but which typically reaches its zenith among the busy middle aged. Meet a mum, any mum, in her forties and in her bag will be a list. Same for men. Well, some men. I know these men. I sit in their offices. These are men who have different sized containers for different sized paperclips next to their phone. COLDists don't just make lists; COLD is about being prescriptively organised. Are you a bit of a

COLDist? Did you write a list on Friday night of things you wanted to achieve over the weekend? Yes? Does this list have a heading? Yes? Is your list headed 'To Do'? Think about this. What are the chances of you writing a list on a Friday night itemising things you want to achieve over the weekend and then rediscovering this list on Saturday morning and thinking, What's all this about? You don't need to put 'To Do' at the top of your list. You'll remember its purpose, I promise. Do you date your lists? Do you have a carry-over policy for items—meaning if you didn't fix the side gate on Saturday, this item reappears on Sunday's list? Or is fixing the side gate a Saturday job, so that this item hibernates until being resuscitated by the list-making process the following Friday night?

Do you know how to freak out a COLDist? I love doing this. You suggest extra things that should be on the list, such as mowing the lawn, and you kindly offer to add this item to the list. If you are truly a COLDist, you will know exactly what is wrong with this suggestion. A hardcore COLDist will never allow anyone to add anything to their list. Why? Different handwriting. It messes with the intrinsic purity of the list: you can't have a list comprised of different voices and different hands. I have seen these multiple-owner lists; they're functional as opposed to pretty. Multiple-owner lists are known among the COLDist set as mongrel lists. And the reason I know about these lists is because on the rare occasion that I do create a list, it is made opportunistically on the back of an envelope without a heading and without the items being numbered. My mongrel lists are a chaotic fusion of unanchored cryptic terms: bread, milk, petrol, side gate. That's it. I don't need a 'To Do' heading and I'm happy if this list is written on the back of an envelope. It's called recycling.

There are other things that trouble the COLDist community. If, for whatever reason, their list isn't long enough— and who doesn't want a long list?—they will add things to that list just so they can be immediately crossed off. Not that true COLDists actually cross things off their lists. Can anyone tell me why? That's right. A line through the words 'Fix the side gate' looks messy. Best to have a system where a task completed is highlighted. And, of course, highlighter-pen cross-offs should never be in mixed colours. Pink is ideal— it suggests stop and that the task has ended—while green highlighter for cross-offs is silly and illogical.

The other thing about COLDists is that they love to show you their list. 'Sorry. Can't stop. I have a list a mile long. See.' I'm not sure what the appropriate response is to being shown a list by a COLDist, but I think it's along the lines of: 'Gosh, you do have a big list, don't you? My list is teeny in comparison. You must be a more successful person than I am because of the length of your list.' If you are a COLDist or even if you have COLDist leanings, I am going to ask that you show tolerance to those of us lesser beings who happily, naively and quite blithely amble through life with list amiss and therefore blissfully listless.

Parisians say *non* to the joy of socks

The French may have loads of *savoir faire* but they need more socks

JE suis a Paris en ce moment. Do you know what I just said? I said I'm in Paris at the moment, on holiday. This experience is not new to me; I have been to Paris several times. Do you know the reason I keep coming back to Paris? For the food? *Non.* Way too rich for *moi.* For the Parisians? Delicate one this one. Look, officially I love the Parisians but I'm not in love with the Parisians. Does that make sense?

No, the reason I keep coming back to Paris for my holidays is to partake of my favourite holiday pastime: people-watching. And in the realm of people-watching, there is no place better than Paris. Consider this. A prime seat in a sidewalk café on fashionable Rue Saint-Honoré with a pot of tea and a macaron on a balmy summer's day with my iPad open to *The Weekend Australian* courtesy of the café's free wi-fi access. Does life get any better than this? I mean seriously. Does it? From this vantage point the whole of life passes you by, from über-chic business-men and high-end fashionistas right through to a random assortment of street show-offs and complete and utter crazies. In other words, nothing unusual.

Now, you may not know this, but I am a bit of a fash-ionista myself. Not in what I wear but very much in what interests me. I like to think that I am up with the latest. And nowhere is the latest more evident than on the streets of Paris. Do you know what smart-set men are wearing in Paris this summer? They're turning up the collar of their sports jackets so as to deliberately expose the felt lining. I should add that the top button of the jacket must be but-toned and a contrasting kerchief should be made to spill jauntily from the breast pocket. But wait, there's more. French fellas are also pushing up their jacket sleeves so as to expose not shirt and cuff but arm and skin. Male fore-arms are boldly and wantonly exposed this summer.

But my eye for male fashion detail goes further. Much fur-ther. Not only are collars being turned up and sleeves being pushed up, but men are wearing shoes without socks. Let me just repeat that: Frenchmen are going sockless. In summer! Now I kinda get the upturned collar thing: it's raffish, it's chic, and I bet it's warm in winter—although I don't think warmth is the purpose of the exercise. But try as I might, I simply do not get the no-sock thing. Perhaps it is just me and my provincial way of thinking, but doesn't anyone else consider that there might be a hygiene issue here? I am all for fashion. But I am also all for cleanliness and no-smelliness.

I know what you're thinking. You're thinking, I bet those French fellas have tiny socklets cut below the ankle. I thought of that too so I studied a few examples. Real hard. One particularly *bon homme* was sitting all cross-legged with a spectacularly naked ankle exposed for all the world to see. And from the angle of my table I had a direct line of sight right into the inside of his shoe. No sock. Nothing. Just bare skin against bare leather. I was shocked. What sort of a person eschews socks? Do Frenchmen think that the sight of a bare ankle, and of a bare forearm for that matter, might attract admiring glances? Excuse me. My glances were different; my glances were research.

Well, let me reassure all those French fashionistas that we Australian men think differently on the subject of socks. We understand the need for socks, the demand for socks, the role of socks—in fact, we understand the joy of socks. In fact so 'for socks' are we Australian men that male grey nomads insist on wearing socks with sandals. Now that is a look that I am sure draws more than a couple of admiring glances from women who think, *Ooh la la*, there's something damned attractive about a man who takes good hygienic care of his feet.

A severe case of melon overkill

There's a conspiracy involving chefs and melon growers and it involves fruit platters

I'M coming straight out with this. I like fruit. In fact, the more I think about it, I'm a bit of a fruitophile. Not a fruito-holic. That would be weird. No, I am a fancier of fruit. Not any fruit, mind you. Fruit must be ripe and piquant; it must be exotic and slightly chilled; but above all it must be untrammelled, unbruised and untouched. Farmers' markets in the south of France sell sun-warmed, ripe fruit. Sorry, but I believe fruit should be firm, chilled and virginal. Indeed, the very idea of eating warm fruit is as unnerving as is sitting on a warm toilet seat; give me the confidence of chilled sterility in both cases every time. I have always liked fruit. Why wouldn't anyone like fruit? It is packed with vitamins and is largely fat-free. And it is so good for you. I am informed that there are internal organs that ben-efit from the passage of fruit. Well, if that is so, then let me assure you that my internal organs must glisten with good health. Just thought I'd share that with you.

Now all of this brings me to my point. Yes, I do have a point and it will arrive shortly. In my travels I stay in swish hotels where I regularly order a fruit platter as part of a meal. Over the years, I have noticed something odd about the average hotel fruit platter. They all have much the same baseload fruit: orange cantaloupe, green honeydew melon and red watermelon. To this base is offered, depend-ing on the swishness of the hotel, a prettily cut orange, a thinly sliced apple or pear, as well as a banana and perhaps a drizzle of passionfruit innards. And then on top—bane of my room-service meal life—a single strawberry replete with intact green-leaf bit.

Fellow fruitophiles will know immediately where I am heading. The only reason honeydew melon and watermelon get a guernsey in a standard fruit platter is not because of any deliciosity factor—yes, there is such a word—but because (a) melons are bulky, common and cheap (sorry, melonophiles, but it's true) and (b) because they can be cut and stacked to deliver baseload fruit. As you can see, I have a lot of time on my hands in hotel rooms to contemplate the structure, form and hidden philosophical meaning of the room-service fruit platter. Rarely do you see interesting fruit such as blueberries and strawberries in fair and equal measure, but rather what you get is boring fruit such as most of the melon family. You do realise that I will receive a letter of complaint this week from the Australian Melon Fanciers' Association.

Let me make this very clear: *j'accuse* five-star hotel kitchen chefs of preferring cheap but visually pleasing melon fruit over expensive but undeniably more delicious berry fruit. In short, my demands of hotel chefs are these: dump the honeydew melon, cut down on the cantaloupe and rid the world of wretched watermelon. Oh, you like watermelon, do you? Well let me tell you something: the only reason watermelon makes it to a summer fruit salad bowl is because it's red and cheap; it's there for its looks, not its substance. This is reverse racism for fruit: watermelon is there because of its colour and bulk. Watermelon is a fruit-salad strawberry or raspberry substitute and everyone knows it.

And while I'm on a roll: that green-leaf thingy bit on top of the strawberry? Why? With all the kitchen gadgetry available to über-chic master chefs, why can't they pluck before they serve? I'll tell you why. Chefs leave the leaf on 'because it looks good'. They like the visual of a voluptuous strawberry being teasingly covered by a skimpy, green, fig-leaf mat. Well, I am so on to you. The green-thingy bit being left on strawberries is emblematic of chefs plating food to please themselves and not the customer. Well, I have had enough: from this day forward, my fruit platter order will specifically request that all strawberry hulls be removed and that the melon content be restricted to no more than 10 per cent of the overall fruit content. And don't think I won't be measuring the melon.

On Planet Tidy, things just add up

Some people can't settle unless everything is on an even keel

YOU know when you set the volume on televisions there is usually a digital scale set from zero to perhaps fifty or 100? Well, do you know there are people in my household who casually and without a care in the world adjust the sound and leave the volume sitting on an odd number? How can anyone sit down to watch *Australia's Funniest Home Videos* with the volume control set to an odd number? The volume should always sit on an even number. It's a matter of tidiness. Surely? I mean, an odd number is just wrong, wrong, wrong. Why, just the other day I turned on the telly and instinctively I knew something was not quite right. And sure enough, not only was the volume sitting on an odd number, it was sitting on number 43. Forty-three! You do realise the significance of 43, don't you? Oh,

I think you do. Forty-three is not only an odd number; it is a prime number. A prime number! You cannot do things with a prime number. Prime numbers just sit there and steadfastly refuse to be divided by any number other than one and themselves. Now that is just plain unfriendly behaviour. On the other hand, a gregarious number such as 48 is—how shall I put this (children might be reading)—much more divisible. Almost every number wants to lustily divide into 48; 4, 8, 6, 2, 12, and I could go on but I think you get my point.

Anyway when I explained my logic about the wrongness of odd numbers and the straight-up weirdness of prime numbers in relation to the TV's volume control, all I got back was a set of incredulous stares and, can you believe it, dropped jaws. I mean, it was as if they thought I was an alien from another planet. Oh, I am an alien from another planet all right. Planet Tidy, where all the numbers behave and none steps out of line. Hmmm, tidy numbers. I like it already. And, in fact, as the Supreme Ruler of Planet Tidy I have decreed that there shall be no prime numbers including that self-absorbed number 1. It's time number 1 got its comeuppance and disappeared: go join the alphabet, number 1; you're such a show-off. Televisions on Planet Tidy have volume controls that can be set only to even numbers: two, four, six, eight, ten and beyond.

Oh yes, yes, yes. Now, I know what you're thinking. You're thinking I'm a Numbers Racist because I don't like odd numbers and I especially don't like unfriendly prime numbers. Well, let me put that one to bed. So to speak. I have always had quite a thing for number 27: three short of 30; easily divisible; two more than 25; comprising a cur-vaceous number 2 and a tick-like number 7. Now that's an attractive number and in fact I defy anyone not to find number 27, ahem, alluring.

So there we go; I like to leave the volume control on even numbers, and unless you want to receive another numbers lecture like this, then it's just easier if everyone on Planet Earth does as we do on Planet Tidy and leave any electronic setting on an even number. Beam me up, Scotty, for my work here is done.

Addicts are hooked up on iPhones

Look, I'm not an iPhone addict but I know people who are

ARE you an iPhone addict? Take a seat and allow me to cross-examine you, your behaviour and your lifestyle. Do you check emails on your iPhone on weeknights when you are home with your family? What about on weekends? Do you zone out of a family conversation to 'just check your emails'? Do you take your iPhone on holidays so you can keep track of what's happening on the work front? Have you checked your iPhone at a family wedding? What about at a funeral? You have, haven't you? Is nothing sacred? Why do you need to look at your iPhone all day, every day? What vital piece of information are you expecting that you have to look at that thing every five minutes?

I know why you do it. It's because work email is intoxicating and addictive. All those permission requests and bits of information being channelled to you from minions and associates in different parts of your business empire: it's information; it's connectivity; it's validation; it's all about you. Email communication is confirmation that you are kingpin (or queen bee) and that you are an essential part of the workplace cognoscenti. Who wouldn't find all this attention flattering?

Of course you have to take your iPhone on holiday; doesn't anyone in this family understand how important you are in the workplace? And it's not as if you respond to monitored email traffic during the weekend; you just like to watch, don't you? It readies you for Monday's onslaught. A weekend isn't for switching off; it's for keeping watch to guard against saboteurs, incompetents and assorted corporate goblins and gremlins who, left unchecked, may upset your stellar trajectory.

When interstate on business and staying at a hotel, do you wake in the night and reach for your iPhone to check the time? And when you check the time do you also think, May as well see what emails have come in? And as you briefly reply to a 2 am email, do you think when you press the send button, I bet they get a surprise at seeing a 2 am time-tag to my reply? This makes you feel all warm and fuzzy inside, so you drop off to sleep in no time, safe in the knowledge you have totally one-upped the sender of the email. I mean, who answers their emails at 2 am? You do, don't you? And you're proud of it, aren't you? Oh yes you are.

When you are at your kid's sport this weekend, will you have your iPhone jammed into your coat pocket ready to respond the second it vibrates? I mean, two hours out in the cold with the ball around your kid for only a few seconds at a time; why not scroll through, review and delete texts so you can make the most of this downtime? You're not being a bad parent; you're just being efficient. Frankly, if the rest of the world were as efficient as you, we'd all be a lot better off. Take your iPhone to junior football? What a fantastic idea. And you know exactly when to look up from the screen because other parents around you start cheering. It's like a nuclear early-warning system. If you do this really well, I reckon you can delude your kid into thinking you are watching the whole match all of the time. You can even listen to the odd voicemail. The other parents aren't going to know; they'll just think you are talking to your partner. Just throw in the odd 'Yes, dear' to throw them off the scent.

What an extraordinary iPhone winner you are. Switched on all day, every day. The nerve centre of a business empire. Then again, you just may be a bit of an iPhone wanker: continually looking at and flicking a screen because you don't have the social skills and the connections to conduct a relationship in the real world outside the workplace. I'm right, aren't I? And if I'm not right, then I am sufficiently close to the truth that you are squirming just a bit. If this is the case, then perhaps it's best that you remain techno-logically cocooned in your workplace because you probably wouldn't survive in the real world, where real people connect in real time.

Dash it, I remain a pedant fan of the comma man

What the world needs now is a better understanding of the semicolon

DO you know the sort of people to whom I am naturally drawn? Okay, so that wasn't too hard: geeks is a good guess, but it's a particular genre of geek that I like. I especially like good or spot-on spellers and pernickety punctuators. In fact, the more pernickety the punctuator the better. There is a punctuation mark that is perfect for every occasion. The fun, the thrill, the adrenalin rush is in dressing otherwise dowdy verbiage with precisely the right punctuation so as to make a sentence sing. And if you cannot relate to what I have just said, then perhaps you and I were never meant to be friends.

I once saw a friend misspell *the Philippines* and I cannot let it go. This person used a double *l* and a single *p*. A double *l* and a single *p*! For *the Philippines*! Ever since *the Philippines* incident, whenever I see this person all I can think about is their embarrassing act of misspelling. Was this carelessness or do they really think this is how *the Philippines* is spelt? What other words don't they know how to spell? Is it wrong to fantasise about giving friends a bit of a spelling bee? Spell *chrysanthemum*; if you can't, then you and I are finished. I can't be friends with a person who can't spell *the Philippines*. What if we are both kidnapped by Filipino separatists holidaying in Australia and smuggled back to the Philippines and held for ransom and my friend gets one chance to send our location to the authorities and misspells *the Philippines* and the person receiving the message is a spelling pedant like me and cannot understand where we are? In that situation I would be a goner and all because I knowingly chose to hang out with a bad speller. Well, that isn't going to happen. Bad speller, be gone.

In the early 1990s I reported to a boss who didn't know the difference between *adverse* (meaning 'inclement') and *averse* (meaning 'disinclined'). And in the late 1980s I had my consulting reports corrected by someone who didn't know the difference between a comma and a semicolon. I mean, really. Needless to say neither of those professional relationships lasted. This raises a delicate issue of workplace manners. Is it acceptable for a junior to correct their superior on matters relating to spelling and punctuation?

I didn't correct semicolon guy at the time, and twenty-plus years later I still ruminate over how I might have tackled him. Look, fella, a comma is most commonly used to separate words in a list or the main clause from the subordinate clause in a sentence. A semicolon, on the other hand, is used to separate independent clauses not conjoined with a coordinating conjunction. How do you think that would have gone down with semicolon guy?

If you really want to get on my good side—and who doesn't?—then I suggest that you find a way to bring into our conversation a way to casually spell out loud the word *confectionery* or the word *stationery*, meaning 'pens and pencils', as opposed to *stationary*, meaning 'still'. Or—and I admit this one is for punctuation pedants only—you could subtly let me know that you know how to correctly use an ellipsis or that you understand the difference between a hyphen and an em dash. Let me say that a friend of mine has quite an eccentric family member who sends emails that are no more than a collection of sentences linked by erratic sequences of three, four and/or five dots. Not only is this a bastardisation of the three-dot ellipsis, it is incorrect usage. The ellipsis signifies interrupted dialogue or the tailing off of a thought into the ... oh never mind. Not only that, but these emails contain multiple exclamation and question marks. Multiple! Doesn't my friend's remote and eccentric family member realise that overuse, let alone multiple use, of such marks cheapens their effect? Nothing packs more punch than a single, well-placed exclamation mark. Nothing! And don't get me started on gen Y's uncritical embrace of the American spellchecker.

Now if you'll excuse me, I have to check and recheck the spelling and punctuation in this column.

Occupational interrogation gives me a chill

Is it mandatory to answer social questions about your occupation?

COME close. I don't want everyone to know what I am about to say. This is between you and me. Right? Just the two of us. Right? Okay. Here goes. I have a phobia. I have a deep-seated fear that will not go away. Do you know what I am scared of? My worst nightmare is being at a party—okay, so I don't go to parties, but you get the idea—and at this party I am introduced to someone who says, 'So, Bernard, what do you do for a living?' I feel like saying, 'Why do you need to know?' Or, 'If I tell you, what are you going to do with the information?' And, you know, I can see them working up to the question. They look you up and down, as if to say, 'Who are you?' Or, 'What are you?' Then they come straight out and ask the question. Were I a school-teacher or a plumber or a lawyer or an accountant, I could answer nonchalantly and move on. But I can't. It's complicated. I didn't set out to make my occupation complicated, but it is. Sorry.

I am often in cabs when, mid-journey, the driver will ask what I do for a living. 'What do you mean what do I do for a living? How is this relevant to the cab ride? Do you ask other passengers what they do for a living? Why me? Do I look shifty?' No, of course I don't say this, but I am thinking this. And I promise I'm not being antisocial. I do understand the need to be pleasant. I can do pleasant. In fact you should see my pleasant. I'll have you know that, when required, I can be downright sociable. So, being sociable, I chat to the driver about the weather or the traffic or the football. You know, the sort of thing that constitutes meaningful verbal exchange between men but which is immediately forgettable.

Recently I have taken to saying that I work for an accounting firm; oddly, that usually stops further questions. Although I did get one driver who wouldn't give up: 'What accounting firm? ... Which area of accounting?' In the end I confessed everything. That cab ride felt like a confessional.

'Look, I don't mean to be evasive but it's not easy explaining what I do. Actually, I work for *The Australian*.'

'So you're a journalist?'

'Not really. I write columns but I also work for an accounting firm, although I'm not an accountant. I trained as a schoolteacher but I never taught. Actually, I'm on the speaking circuit. Oh, and occasionally I write books. Okay, okay, here's the deal: I'm a cross between a journalist, a business adviser, a corporate speaker, an author and a media commentator. That's the sum of what I do, okay? Are you happy? Now can you please take me to St Leonards?'

Do other people have this problem? Why is it relevant to ask a person's occupation? It doesn't occur to me to ask you your occupation. Why do you need to know mine? It's akin to asking someone their religion. 'So, you're Jewish, are you?'

'No.'

'Catholic? I knew it.'

I suspect it's all part of the social stratification process: lawyer beats accountant beats schoolteacher. Not that I think that, but I suspect that's what people who ask others their occupation are thinking. I also have this sneaking suspicion that the occupation question is a proxy for 'How much do you earn?' The more socially acceptable way to manage this is to ask someone where they live. And often the name of the suburb is not enough. I mean, genuine riffraff can live in an apartment in Toorak, so you need to know precisely which street and whether it's a good street. 'Oh, Toorak, how lovely. I have so many friends there. Where are you?' And if you say Toorak Road, which is a bit like New South Head Road or Military Road in Sydney, then the inquisitor will know that you are in fact nothing more than a flat-dwelling pretender and that they have just gazumped you in a rollicking session of the social stratification game.

3

Manners and Mores

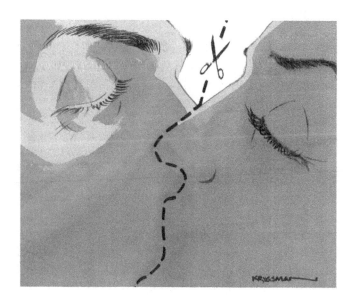

NO argument is required on the issue of manners and mores. It is a fact that much of what passes through the average person's mind involves daily musing about—perhaps even fuming over—the manners, or the lack thereof, of others. The manners of others can indeed be a decent obsession. Are you confronted by a couple kissing passionately—I mean really going for it—in public? No? Neither am I. But does it make a difference if that couple is middle-aged as opposed to young and passionately reckless? Officially I say no, but practically I say yes. Put a lid on it!

But being irked by the manners of others goes beyond public displays of middle-aged affection. It extends to the unfortunately not-so-rare creatures who do not keep appointments and who see no need to inform other parties to that appointment that their plans have changed.

How much brain space is devoted to being agitated by the behaviour of others? This of course raises the question of whether everyone thinks that it is other people who are ill mannered. Regardless, evidence abounds of minds being consumed by the manners and mores of others; this includes egregious examples of people who deliberately and with malice aforethought eat and speak loudly in public and/or who gesticulate wildly in a public place. And all of course to the unspoken disapproval of the polite, who silently plan speeches that are never delivered. This is not so much a matter of whether these examples are fair or unfair; it is a matter of whether we are easily preoccupied—even obsessed—with the manners and mores of others.

No need to make a pash of it

I'm all for kissing in public but I draw the line at a full-on pash by a middle-aged couple

THERE I was minding my own business walking down the street when there, slap bang in the middle of the road, was a couple. Kissing! Now I know that you think I'm a raving conservative, but let me assure you I am very much in favour of public displays of affection. But when I say public displays of affection, I don't mean gratuitous and graphic displays of affection; I mean sensible, mature, tempered, corralled, manacled displays of affection. Actually, can you scrap manacled? I am quite a fan of public displays of affection. You know, the way Prince Charles, lovingly I might add, still greets his sons with a kiss on the cheek. I love that.

But having said all of this, there are a couple of points you need to appreciate about the PKI, or public kissing incident. This wasn't a 'Hi, how are you?' kiss on the cheek; this was a full-on, head-moving, eyes-closed, arm-gripping, oblivious-to-the-world, prolonged pash. Thank you; I thought exactly the same. There is a time and a place, and Melbourne's Flinders Lane at 10 am on a weekday is neither the time nor the place.

But wait, there's more. This was not a hormone-charged young couple exuberantly celebrating and barely containing an amorous moment. This was—hushed tone—an older couple. No, not old old, just old. You thought I meant old old, didn't you? An old old couple kissing like that in a public street! What are you? Sick? No, she was in her late thirties and he must have been over fifty. Over fifty! I mean he was balding and paunchy. There are some who believe that paunchy, middle-aged people should keep all but polite air kissing very much to themselves. But even when this lot does get involved in polite air kissing, it's generally preferred that they not allow their lips to connect with any of the exposed cheek surface area of the person they are greeting.

Actually, why stop at the middle-aged and the paunchy? The entire race of generation Y believe to their core that also on the banned list of who can and who cannot indulge in public displays of over-the-top affection are parents. Generation Y's parents are henceforth banned from all public acts of kissing other than for the obligatory good-morning-dearest peck on the cheek. Don't make me spell out the full range of activities that are on the parents' banned list, but I think you get the general idea. Basically the principle is that nothing should, you know, 'happen' between parents in a public setting that is likely to embarrass or disgust teenage children, or any of their friends and associates, or anyone who goes to their school. Or indeed anyone whom they pass on their way to school. And I might add that this audience—teenage children—is highly critical of errant parental behaviour. Yes, Mum and Dad, holding hands is acceptable. Although this hand-holding specifically excludes any actions involving or leading to the highly suggestive interlocking of fingers. I think we all know what's going on when that happens!

So there you have it. Public displays of affection involving kissing are in fact permitted among amorous young couples aged 18–23. But thereafter the rules tighten progressively such that the middle-aged, as well as those in their late-twenties and the old old, are at liberty to display affection. It's just that they have to make sure that it's never too much affection. Just like the middle-aged couple I saw kissing in the street: terrific stuff, but either tone it down in public or please take it inside.

Irked by stand-up routines

Some people break time commitments without the slightest care

HELLO dearest readers. Ssshh. Before you answer, can I ask you to keep your voice down? I don't want the world to know what I am about to tell you. It's important that you act natural. If you are reading this in a trendy café with a caffè latte (with barista-designed froth) could I suggest that you breezily look up from the paper and signal for yet another low-fat biscotti from the waiter. No sudden movements or you'll give the game away. The reason for all this subterfuge is that I don't want you to tip 'them' off, once I reveal what I have to reveal. The 'them' to whom I refer are, of course, an uncannily humanoid life form that has taken root in modern society. I suspect they come from another planet—probably one of Jupiter's moons—and although I know not the purpose of their visit to our fair planet, I can tell you that I am familiar with their bent ways.

I am referring to people who happily and without conscience distort what we Earthlings call 'time' and 'commitment'. When an Earthling like me says to another Earthling like you, 'I'll meet you at 11 am', do you know what I do? Well, at 10.45 I think, I've made a commitment to meet someone at 11, so if I want to fulfil that commitment I'll have to get a wriggle on. Or, if I cannot make that commitment, I think, I'll use this thing called a telephone to call ahead and explain what's happened. Now, oddly, this logic doesn't seem to apply on the planet these humanoid aliens come from. They think it's rather jolly and fun to say, 'Yep, I'll meet you at 11' and then when that hour comes around they think … they think … well, no one really knows what they think because they offer no explanation. Isn't that extraordinary? In fact, the whole arrangement is erased from their memory banks. Isn't that convenient? There is no guilt because the commitment did not and does not exist.

And when you question these people about their 11 am commitment, it's like, 'Yeah? So? I had stuff come up.' Oh, well, that explains everything if, you know, you have stuff that comes up. I mean, you cannot be expected to think about a commitment or to ring ahead if stuff comes up. But here's the thing. Stuff can come up for humanoid time-and-commitment aliens, but it does not come up for Earthlings like you and me. Or if stuff does come up, we Earthlings deal with it and—here's a novel concept—we manage the situation and the expectations of the person to whom the commitment has been given.

Have you ever been caught in this situation? Because if you have, then you, too, have had a brush with an alien life form. In fact, so prevalent is this lack of commitment to time and arrangements that I suspect the aliens' mothership is hovering over Antarctica. What else could explain why so many seem to be living in Australia? Of course, this is one perfectly logical explanation. The other is that we are evolving into an extraordinarily self-centred nation, interested only in ourselves to the extent we do not care if someone has been 'stood up'. I'd rather think that there is a mothership from Jupiter hovering over

Antarctica than accept the possible, and more probable, explanation that many in this nation are growing more self-centred every day.

Blokes let their hands do the talking

The handshake for men can say so much about a relationship

DO you know one of the biggest differences between men and women? It's in the deployment of greeting options for people of the same sex. Same-sex greeting protocols are far more interesting than the vexed issue of same-sex marriage, don't you think? Consider the evidence. Women greeting women have the handshake for formal occasions and the full-on air kiss and hug for friends and family. Men on the other hand have fewer options when it comes to the tricky business of greeting other men. It's pretty much the handshake and nothing else. And it's a protocol that applies universally, even to closely related males such as, for example, middle-aged fathers and adult sons.

Now you might think that this is all just so typical of men: absolutely no creativity. But if you did think this way, then you would be wrong, because over the centuries we men have been silently, diligently, sensitively working on a secret project. Yes, I am about to expose to the world the highly complex, sophisticated, but above all silent communication that takes place within the confines of the manly man-to-man handshake. Now this communication has nothing to do with fancy American subculture handshakes that require a sequence of moves. No. This involves the subtle world of the Australian male handshake, where to the untrained eye a handshake might look like a handshake. But to male participants in handshake-events this is an ancient ritual that often involves a man-to-man conversation of which women are unaware. Until now that is. Hold on to your hats, ladies, because this is going to get pretty rugged. And that's rugged with a capital *R*. Ha. We men have been talking to each other about all sorts of stuff through our handshakes and women have had absolutely no idea what's been goin' on. And to be frank, we men are pretty pleased with ourselves for keeping it secret for such a long time.

For example, ladies, do you know why men stick out their hand well in advance of meeting other men? It's so we can line each other up in order to get the proper palm-thumb connection required for the ensuing shake. We like to pretend we are space stations docking. And as every male knows, you need a jolly good connection to deliver a jolly good docking. And if the docking goes particularly well, we like to transmit to each other, through a chemical process known as masculine osmosis, the following: 'Hmmm, good docking; no girly tip-of-the-fingers grip; manly shake; I can do business with you.' And the other bloke is likely to transmit much the same. See? Complete conversation.

Then of course there is the shake itself. Now again to women looking on they probably think, Huh, handshake. Boring. Nothing to see here. But again women would be wrong. The rules of the shake are: one move up and one move down, then you let the hand go. But that's not all. At precisely mid-shake, there is an accompanying head nod. Not a shake but a nod. Not two nods (that would be, like, weird) but one. But wait, there's more. While simultaneously executing the handshake and the head-nod—are you keeping up ladies?—there should be a single utterance of the handshakee's name, as in, 'Bernard'. Three moves at once ladies; how impressive is that? It is important that while the shakee's name is being uttered, the utterer's lips should not move. The word 'Bernard' must merely emit from the general head precinct of the utterer. Yes, it's known in male circles as the Ventriloquist's Addendum to the Handshake Convention and its purpose is as important as it is simple. If women in the vicinity were to cotton on to the fact that we men were actually talking to each other, then they would ask all sorts of questions, such as 'What did you chat about?' And as all male signatories to the Handshake Convention know, we don't want women to know exactly how sensitive and communicative we really are.

Scrambled, beaten and flushed ...

Please eat with your mouth shut. Please.

I HAVE decided I am not for this world. Either that or it's the end of the year and I have had it up to here with the rest of humanity. There I am in a five-star hotel on a Sunday having breakfast and reading the papers, and a couple in their sixties sit at the next table. As I sip my tea I become aware of a background noise that is gathering pace and volume. What is that macabre jungle sound that beats towards me? A *clink clink, knyack knyack* sound. I swivel slightly in my chair and there in full flight is this couple eating loudly. Eating loudly! Scrambled eggs! Scrambled eggs? Why is it necessary to clink a knife and fork into scrambled eggs? Scrambled eggs do not require cutting with such force that the knife is clinked into the china plate below. Or is my experience with scrambled eggs different from that of everyone else? And the *knyack knyack*? Well, that is of course the disgusting sound of scrambled eggs being masticated by an open-mouthed chewer. I could perhaps, perhaps, forgive this in a child. But this *clink clink*, shovel shovel, *knyack knyack* from sixty-somethings is intolerable. If I am ever thrown into Guantanamo Bay and interrogated by the CIA, they would not have to look far to find my weakness. Just have one of their burly agents sit down in front of me to eat scrambled eggs in a disgusting manner and I would divulge everything. Everything. Just make the noise stop.

If this inability to cope with what can only be described as the disgustingness of others was a one-off, I wouldn't be so worried. But I seem to be surrounded. Do you think there is a Secret Society for the Disgusting that has targeted me? I don't think so. I know so. They have agents everywhere. How about earlier in the year while I was at the washbasin in a public bathroom and a mobile phone rang out from inside one of the cubicles? Not that this is unusual. Phones have a habit of ringing at the darnedest of times. It will ring out or the owner will turn it to silent. Surely. You know what is coming next, don't you?

'Hello.'

Sure enough, what ensued was the onset of a full-on conversation. Or at least I assume it was a full-on conversation because I didn't stick around to listen in. Not that I would have had to listen hard, because this conversation was being transmitted to the entire bathroom from deep inside that cubicle. As I left the bathroom, a number of philosophical questions sprang to mind: Is there a moral ethical obligation by a called person to inform the caller of their circumstances? Is there a hygiene issue in handling a mobile phone from inside a toilet cubicle? Does it make a difference if it's not a hand-held phone but a Bluetooth earpiece? Who cares: why would anyone conduct a telephone conversation from within a public toilet? And yet people clearly do. And it bothers me.

I have no idea who is behind the Secret Society for the Disgusting, but they are doing a fantastic job in promoting their evil cause. I suspect all of this stems from a shift in our collective thinking. For more than half a century we have been told we are special to such a degree that the individual no longer has 'vision' of anyone else. All we can see now is ourselves. If you are at the centre of society, then you are not obligated to think about anyone else. And this means you can eat scrambled eggs as loudly as you wish, and you can conduct an animated telephone conversation from inside a toilet cubicle. But it doesn't make it right. Please, please make the *knyack knyack* sound stop.

Not waving, drowning in gestures

Why can't gesticulators do their gesticulating in private?

SO there I am checking into the business lounge at Melbourne airport and as I glance into the distance I see a man waving to me. My eyesight isn't what it used to be so I can't quite make out who it is. He is standing facing me, waving. He must know me well because he has the nter: one hand by his side and the other gorous wave. I am clearly being engaged ure, not on a grassy knoll but near the tation. I just hope I can remember his name before I get up to him. You know how it goes. 'Oh, hello …' (and in the nanosecond that follows you pray that he says, 'Bernard, it's Barry'). 'Yes of course, Barry. How are you?'

So it is with some trepidation that I man up to the gunslinger, hoping to get a clue as to who knows me so well that he would wave vigorously from across a crowded room. Normally blokes don't do vigorous waves to other blokes; we're more inclined to nod, and if we know each other well, we might mouth each other's name and then move on. Otherwise we might get involved in an unnecessary conversation. And if there's one thing blokes do not do, it is unnecessary conversation. Men are hunters. Hunters no talk. Men no talk. Men nod. Men mouth name if necessary. Which way men's room? So you can see the significance of a full-on wave. But as I approach the gunslinger he turns his back on me. He does not know me. He does not want to know me. And as it happens I do not know him. He has a Bluetooth earpiece in his ear and he was on the phone gesticulating wildly. I mistook his gesticulation for a wave and like a giddy schoolgirl I shot back a wave. Well, I felt used.

This happened a year ago and as you can see I am still smarting. Who is this person who has stolen my wave? I am not the sort of person who goes around giving waves to everyone. I filter my wave partners very carefully. Waving is a two-way street, you know. I can't be all giving out waves willy-nilly and then getting no waves in return. That's emasculating. And this, of course, brings me to my point. Why is it necessary for Bluetooth people to gesticulate wildly and to talk loudly on the phone? I am always on my phone and I speak quietly and with only a modicum of gesticulation.

I have a theory. I suspect that Bluetooth people are so chuffed by their bluetoothosity that they want the world to see and acknowledge their superior telecommunication skills. That's why they gesticulate. It's a look-at-me gesture that is often accompanied by a bizarre snippet of a conversation that everyone can hear: 'Yeah, well you tell Dicko that if he doesn't accept my offer I'm walkin'. Got that? Tell Dicko I'm walkin'.' Gosh, I wouldn't want to be in Dicko's shoes. But what possible conversations require a both-arms-outstretched gesticulation? 'Hey, Dicko, mate, I caught a whopper on the weekend and it was this big.'

Whereas we Luddites who still hold a phone to our ear can only gesticulate with one hand. We could never indicate the size of a fish because our limited command of technology restricts us to one-handed stories. 'Dicko, mate, when conducting the overture you can move the baton up and down and sometimes sideways.' You see, we phone-Luddites are limited in the things that we can talk about because we have only one arm free.

Do you think it is rude to suggest that Bluetooth phone users restrict their wild gesticulations to private as opposed to public spaces? And while I'm on the subject, would they and others also mind keeping their public telephone conversations private? Not only is it annoying, but I remain completely unsatisfied by the snippets of conversation that I overhear. Did Dicko accept? Did Bluetooth gesticulator man walk? We will never know.

Modern manners go out the window

Sadly manners seem to be out of fashion

DO you know what I can't stand? Bad manners, especially in people who should know better. At the upper echelon of business, for example, there are some people who do not return phone calls. It's a power kick. You call and leave a message and they decide whether to speak to you. And if they determine you are of no use to them, your call is ignored. You learn gradually, painfully, during the next twenty-four hours, that you have been dismissed: go away and don't come back until you are vaguely interesting.

Or how about when you are at an airline check-in desk and you ask about changing your flight and the attendant barely acknowledges your existence before putting his head down and beginning to type. And type. And all done without saying a word. How about saying hello? How about saying: 'I'm just searching availability'? How about keeping me informed as to what is happening? How about acknowledging my existence?

What about when you are at a drinks function and people are gathered in tight circles so that anyone unknown to the group is excluded? Or how about when you do speak to someone at a drinks function and they look beyond you for more interesting people to chat to? Or does this only happen to me because I am the most boring person in the world? Or how about in economy class on planes (yes, I travel economy) when the person in front pushes their seat back without so much as an 'Excuse me' or 'Do you mind?'

Why is it that I cannot do any of these things? I cannot but return a phone call even if it takes a day to find the time. I cannot push my seat back in a plane without turning and saying 'Do you mind?' to the person behind. I cannot chat in a tight circle of business people and not include someone who obviously doesn't know anyone. Why can't I do any of this? I'll tell you why. It's because I have decided that I am the only normal person on this planet. Okay, so you are normal, too. That makes two of us out of seven billion people. Everyone else is rude and selfish and, frankly, should have been taught better manners when they were growing up.

But this isn't the end of it. Bad manners reach their zenith at the dinner table. I have been at enough lunches and dinners to know that even the most sophisticated people don't seem to know how to hold a knife and fork. Fingers should not touch the fork's tines or the back of the knife's blade. You should not speak to just one person for the entire meal. Speak to the person at your left during entree and to the person at your right during mains. How about when you are at a dinner on a rectangular table and you have the end seat? If the person in the second-last seat doesn't engage with you, then you are left sitting like a shag on a rock with no one to talk to. Doesn't the second-last seated person see this? Why is it that I see a moral and ethical duty to include such people cut off by table geography from the rest of the conversation?

On the issue of bad table manners, could I just say that there is a special category for Americans. I do not like, but

I understand and accept, their unusual custom of using the fork like a shovel. A shovel! What I cannot stand is the way they, and increasingly some Australians, eat fast food: in the street, on the go, with an open-mouthed chewing action. If you can bear to look, you can actually see food rolling around like the inside of a cement mixer!

And I haven't even got on to the subject of gum-chewing or disgusting personal habits such as sniffing. Do serial sniffers think that no one can hear them? Not only can I hear you, Mr Serial Sniffer, but it takes my entire willpower not to offer you a box of tissues and tell you to please blow your nose. In the middle of a business meeting! If you, like me, are one of the rare people who see flaws like this everywhere, then I invite you to join me in my newly formed Society for Normal People. For it is only we, at the society, who seem to appreciate the value of good manners.

Yes, the wretched food is just fine, thanks

Diners are receiving incessant requests for praise

SOMETHING isn't quite right in the restaurant business and hasn't been right for quite some time. I am referring to the practice of the waiter or the maître d' or the owner or all three approaching diners to ask if everything is to their satisfaction.

Now you probably think I'm being pernickety; this is a lovely thing for a business to do. But I promise I am not being pernickety: there is a fine line between polite diner enquiry and incessant requests for validation. This has gone beyond a 'How are things going?' sort of chat. Rather this has moved into the sphere of an interrogation: 'Tell me the raw, primal, guttural emotion that you feel as you eat—no, strike "eat"; make that "experience"—this restaurant's food (strike "food"; make it "gastronomic art").' What is it with this generation of service providers that they expect constant validation? 'Look, fella, can't you just accept that I am in your restaurant eating your overpriced, small-portioned but prettily arranged food? Isn't that enough?' During the meal I am now apparently required to deliver a heart-warming story about how my life has been changed by the food, the service, the atmosphere that pertains to this sacred place, which some philistines call a restaurant but which we all know should be referred to as a Temple of Taste. 'But, fella, I have only just sat down. How can I legitimately tell you how wonderful you are as a waiter, as a chef, as a culinary institution within five minutes of sitting down? Go away. I am not your friend. I am a customer who is paying for a service. I am not a groupie looking for an opportunity to stroke your ego. Sorry.'

A few weeks ago, I was in a smart restaurant in Melbourne's leafy eastern suburbs early in the evening—6.30 pm (so I like to eat early)—and after taking my order, the waiter hung around for a chat: 'Where are you from?' 'How come you're here early?' Then the owner walked up for a chat: 'Where did you park?' 'Are you in a rush?' I am a big boy. I can manage the parking situation. If I need to get somewhere, I will tell you. I am sure these people were bored waiting for the evening to start; they presumed that I'd be up for a chat because, well, they are food artistes and everyone wants to chat with a food artiste, don't they?

Does anyone else think that the whole restaurant/café world is starting to take on the sort of self-absorption that pertains to the acting industry? These people get paid to do a job; they do their job; then they want an award and/or some sort of recognition for doing their job. There are no Academy awards or Logies for plumbers. A plumber understands that they are paid to do a job. A plumber does not then expect validation from the client as to the creative way that they completed the job. 'Bazza, I just want to say that the soldering job you did on that copper connection has changed my life. I especially enjoyed your deft use of flux.'

Is this the outcome of a generation whose every action has been feted? It is no longer sufficient to merely give someone your business; now they also expect personal validation. Restaurant menus often state that there is a surcharge on public holidays. They should also state that in addition to the monetary cost the operators also reserve the right to apply a Validation Levy where the diner is required to say nice things about the food and the restaurant. The Validation Levy is often randomly applied during the meal. When it is applied, diners are required to stop whatever conversation they are engaged in, look up, smile and say something nice. If the collector of the Validation Levy is satisfied that the statements offered have been sufficiently sycophantic, the collector will leave the diners in peace. If the validation offered is deemed to have been under par, the collector hangs around until what is known as the Validation Threshold has been met. If you ever want the maître d' to move on, then use the phrase 'This menu is inspirational' as opposed to 'Yeah, good thanks', which is no longer sufficient praise in a world obsessed with validation culture.

Mind your manners

Corporates can be rude when rejecting a job application

IS there such a thing as corporate rudeness? Or, more fairly, a lack of care, consideration and manners by business? And by business I also mean government departments. Perhaps the best example of what I'm talking about involves job applications.

I have heard horror stories of job advertisements requiring the preparation of a CV, the writing of a cover letter and no less than one and sometimes multiple interviews, as well as psychological testing, that end up in the candidate being rejected without so much as an email, let alone a phone call, to explain the outcome. Perhaps I'm old-fashioned, because I think that if someone has put effort into a solicited application then the least they can expect in return is acknowledgement of receipt of the application and, if unsuccessful, timely advice to that effect. It would be especially helpful if the rejection letter or email (or preferably phone call) gave a generic clue as to the reason. 'We went with someone with more experience.' Great. You gave it a go. You were unsuccessful. You understand why. You can get on with your life.

It's not a good look to ignore people who've genuinely put in effort. And apart from that, it's just plain inconsiderate to hold someone in abeyance, to leave them hanging. How hard is it to send a group email to unsuccessful candidates? It's easy. Just press send. Do it!

Now I do get this from a corporate point of view: perhaps several people were involved in the interviewing process and each thought that someone else was letting unsuccessful candidates know. The group approach allows those with a job to off-load responsibility to someone else. Not my fault!

In today's world of social media and cultivated corporate images I'm surprised a whiz-bang gen-Y tech-head hasn't devised a system by which businesses can be rated on how they treat not so much the successful candidate but multiple unsuccessful ones, who then happily discuss their experience with friends and family and anyone else who'll listen. This should not be a forum for the disaffected and the disgruntled to sound off but a tool to give voice to the genuinely disempowered. I am no gen-Y tech-head, as you may have gathered, so I have set up a Facebook page, Society for Business Courtesy (SBC), to encourage better business manners so that all job applicants are treated, at the very least, with respect and courtesy. I have no problem with not replying to an unsolicited submission. But if a job is advertised, then all applicants—the successful and the unsuccessful—should be treated with the same respect.

And while I'm on a roll, I also think there should be a filtered version of something like seek.com.au to identify jobs that require no experience. One of the problems with the labour market is getting novice workers into the workforce. Which employers are prepared to give young people a go, straight out of university or trade school or Year 10? Again, the request for experience is all very well if you are in the workforce. But what if you're not? How diminishing is this for smart young kids: to pore through job site after job site, only to be disheartened by the incessant demand for experience? And then, when they do send in an application, there's often no acknowledgement, let alone a reply that they've been unsuccessful.

Not all corporates, businesses and government departments are guilty of this seeming lack of concern, but I suspect many are. Let's change the culture; let's encourage the business community to be mindful of how people feel when applying for jobs. Join my Facebook page Society for Business Courtesy (SBC) and be part of the manners revolution.

4

Everyday and Ordinary

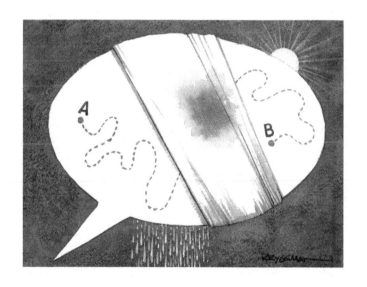

THERE are some things that preoccupy the mind that float in and that float out. Perhaps it is no surprise that it is, or that it should be, the ordinary and the everyday that dominate day-to-day thinking. Have you ever stopped to think how often the egg ring in the kitchen implement drawer is actually used? Do you ever forget someone's name and, in wracking your mind, you recall their children's names, their husband's name, their address and what their house looks like—in fact everything other than their actual name? And do you then scheme as to how you can get through a conversation with that person without disclosing the fact that you've forgotten their name? No? Neither have I. But I know people like this. Have you ever thought about the number of pillows on your bed and how they came to take up residence? Do you find some words pleasing to the ear? Do you ever deliberately include words in your speech for no other reason than such words are pleasing? Have you ever wondered why it is that the office biscuit barrel never contains the more delicious biscuits—specifically Butternut Snaps—no matter how early in the morning you have a cup of tea? Do you find yourself wondering whether there isn't a biscuit barrel conspiracy in your workplace? No? Neither do I. But I'm sure some people do. And if some people do think like this, then they are clearly preoccupied with matters of minutiae that somehow seem to matter.

You can say that again

It's time for a cuppa and a chat

I WAS in Sydney last week. Had a cup of tea with someone I hadn't seen in ten years. Apparently—apparently—Sydney is having an unusually wet winter. Yes. But then, I suppose the rain makes farmers happy. And it's good for the roses, too. Although not too much rain, as that brings out black spot.

Are you getting an insight into the sparkling conversational topics that are in store for you should you find yourself in a small-talk situation with me? Or indeed with pretty much anyone over the age of fifty? How do you know you have progressed beyond the point of no return into the land of the middle-aged? The first item on the agenda is weather. Although I will concede there is a uniquely male variation on the ever-popular weather theme that is known in conversational circles as TPD, or traffic, parking and directions. Isn't the traffic bad? Where did you park? And my personal favourite: which way did you come? This is pure conversational gold for men uncomfortable with unstructured chitchat.

'Got a park straight outside.'

'No! You didn't!'

'Absolutely. And I took the beach road, which was a bit of a gamble this time of night, but it was a good run.'

Now I do understand that to persons of the female sex this might seem like a mundane exchange, but let me assure you that we men see endless possibilities in this conversation.

'The beach road, eh? Cops had a breathalyser there last week. I'd had a few, but they waved me through.'

'No!'

'Yep.'

You do realise I could go on, but I could end up disclosing all my male small-talk secrets, and then I would have to kill you.

Do you know the next most popular item on the over-fifties' conversational agenda? Ailments. Not your ailments. My ailments. Very popular item, this one. Here's how it works. Basically I want to tell you about my ailment but I understand the need for conversational balance, so after I tell you about my ailment I'll listen to you tell me about your ailment. But if your ailment is more dramatic than my ailment, then I'll have to upscale with an even more serious ailment or, better still, I'll have to recount the circumstances that led to my recent or upcoming medical procedure. I have recently had laser eye surgery so I am right on trend here. I can out-ailment anyone on this subject because I am, like, totally across this procedure: they knock you out; they fix your eyes; you wake up. Now that's interesting. Are you calling out for more? I hear you. Two years ago I had a bilateral (always good to use medico language where possible) knee arthroscopy (oh yes, another medico term. I am flyin' here).

Who would want to be in their forties, talking about boring topics such as careers and kids' schooling? Although I must say there is one forty-something conversation topic that is ghoulishly riveting: the breakdown of other people's marriages. And the more spectacular the circumstances, the better. Apparently—apparently—he caught them (hushed tone) *in flagrante delicto*. Conversation in the thirties depends which tribe you belong to. The family-formation tribe talks of children and 'renos', which as we all know is thirty-something-speak for renovations. Then there's the singles tribe, whose obsession is relationships. Who is seeing whom, basically. Where the term *seeing* is a euphemism for 'sleeping with', and which is entirely necessary because you can't really say so and so is sleeping with such and such. Can you?

I wonder what's in conversational store for the sixties. Oddly enough, I suspect that the weather will not only still be in vogue in the sixties but that it will gather conversational momentum. Men in their sixties buy rain gauges and they feel compelled to tell you how much rain they got last night. I must be years off sixty because I haven't the slightest urge to buy a rain gauge. As yet.

Hello, my name is ... um ... er ...

The perils of forgetting someone's name

I SHOULDN'T be telling you this because one day we might meet and it could make things difficult. I suffer from an affliction known as delayed memory response, or DMR syndrome. No, this is not an official medical term because I have just made it up. But it should be a medical condition. With its own Latin name.

There I am at the supermarket and I make eye contact with a woman whom I know but whose name just will not come to me. Not to worry because it's merely a nod and smile from across the oranges display. But what if she walks over? Is she manoeuvring her trolley to walk over? She is walking over! Why can't she be satisfied with a nod and a smile? I do a really nice nod and smile. I raise my eyebrows, give a bit of a wave of my right hand and I mouth the word 'Hi'. Oh, what is her name? Our kids went to primary school together. I was on a school fete stall with her years ago. She wore a designer apron; lawyer husband; very tall; two kids; very sporty. Oh, what is the use of knowing extraneous detail when I can't remember her name? I can't say, 'Hello Ms Lawyer-Husband-with-Two-Kids.'

I need to buy time. If she says, 'Hello, Bernard,' I'll deflect by saying, 'Fancy running into you here' and then I'll follow up by asking about each family member by name so that she couldn't possibly think that I have forgotten her name. I mean if I know her husband's name and her kids' names then surely I must know her name. Maybe when I get into the conversation her name will come to me and I can backfill by inserting her name into the chat. Jane! It's Jane. She looks like a Jane. No, it's not Jane. Amanda? No, it's definitely a single-syllable name. Fiona? Fiona has three syllables! Focus, Bernard, focus. It's no use. I'm just trawling middle-class girls' names from the 1960s. Gail? Is Gail a one- or two-syllable name, because I'd argue it's one syllable that's been stretched. Bernard, you are wasting time and she-who-is-yet-to-be named is getting closer. Uh-oh, she is smiling. She is going to say my name. I know she is going to say my name. She is beyond the oranges and is already at the avocados. Please don't say my name, lady.

'Hello, Bernard, how are you?'

It's my worst nightmare. I can't fake it. I can't ask her her name because we know each other so well. But if I know her so well, then why can't I remember her name? But it's not my fault. I am meeting her out of context. But my local supermarket is context. I have no plausible excuse for forgetting her name. Eventually it'll come to me. Possibly in the car park as I am leaving the supermarket. If it does, I'm going to wait till she comes out then I'll drive past, wind down the window and say goodbye, so-and-so. Oh God, it's been a three full nanoseconds since she said 'Hello, Bernard'; I can't stall any longer. Or can I? I love the music they play in this supermarket; do you think I could ask management for the name of the CD? What am I doing? Focus, Bernard.

'Oh, hi, how are you?'

Pathetic. You paused. She knows. And what's more, she knows that you know she knows. Do you think it's the onset of Alzheimer's? It's the Gypsy Kings. Why can't mainstream supermarkets play the Gypsy Kings instead of Muzak? And why am I impressed with the Gypsy Kings? They're so last decade? Or was it the decade before? Is this the way memory degeneration starts? Between the oranges and the avocados? If my forgetfulness was a recognised medical condition I could have just said, 'Oh, hi, how are you? Look, I'm terribly sorry but my DMR is playing up: what's your name?' And she would have said, 'No worries, Bernard. It's Jill.' And I would have said, 'Of course, Jill. How are you?' But sadly DMR sufferers get no concession for their affliction so we suffer in silence. Mind you, Jane was a pretty close guess, don't you think?

In praise of euphonious word relics

Some words are simply far more attractive than others

THERE is something you should know about me: I am a collector of words. Not just any words—where's the fun in that? I am a collector of beautiful, old and rarely used words. I don't mind the occasional foreign word—adds a bit of piquancy, a bit of pizzazz—but they must have some resonance in English. I'm like a collector of teapots. I hunt them down and store them in a glass cabinet where I can admire their beauty and their, ahem, rhythmic form.

Take, for example, one of my favourite words these days: *rigmarole*. Like most people, I have no idea what a rigmarole is but I like its form—rig-ma-role—and I love the fact no one knows what it is. Did you know that rigmarole can be accessed only by key words: *whole* and *great*, as in 'the whole rigmarole' or 'a great rigmarole'. Isn't that interesting? I am also quite partial to *shebang*. What is a shebang, and is it related to rigmarole, since both refer to much the same thing? Clearly the English language is deficient in words needed to describe large and unwieldy concepts. *Shebang* also has an access word, as in 'the whole shebang'. Like *rigmarole*, *shebang* cannot survive in isolation. Then there's *kit and caboodle*. I think I know what a kit is, but what's a caboodle, and can it exist without kit?

Now we're getting to the heart of my collection. When I was about fifteen, I heard someone make reference to something they thought was tickety-boo. Tickety-boo? Generation Y, did you know there is a word in the English language called *tickety-boo*? I haven't heard it since, other than in movies, although this might tellingly mean that no one in my presence has ever thought everything was tickety-boo. I am so non-tickety-boo. What does it mean? Well, when a circumstance is just right, it is said to be tickety-boo. From what strange source did tickety-boo derive, or is it the linguistic detritus of some previous civilisation?

Then, of course, there are foreign words that have been pressed into common usage. I especially like *bushido* and *bravado*, which I know have slightly different meanings, but since one is from Japan and the other from Spain, don't you think it's interesting that they sound alike and refer to more or less the same thing? I love the word *insouciance* and especially as it is pronounced by the French (in-soo-shongce), but so few people know its meaning ('carefree') that I am embarrassed to use it in everyday language. Maybe I can meet other word lovers and we could talk without shame in our secret collectable word language.

Not only do I collect words that have something interesting to say, but I also collect words that sound pretty. Some words are collectable not for their intellectual contribution but because of their beauty and their voice. I especially like typing an unusual word into my computer and having it sail straight through spell-check. Oh yeah, I can spell *insouciance* without any help. I like words with a pleasing rhythm. Tell me that you too don't get a frisson of pleasure every time you order the phonetically delectable, not to mention delicious, san choy bow in a Chinese restaurant. I also like referring to Burmese Nobel laureate Aung San Suu Kyi, which in pronunciation rolls off the tongue like rich warm honey: 'aung san suu chi, aung san suu chi'. I even like pronouncing the name of the Indonesian President, Susilo Bambang Yudhoyono, which is so much more arresting than SBY, don't you think? My question is this: is it wrong for me to say out loud my various collectable words and other people's names merely for my own pleasure? I am sure Aung San Suu Kyi and Susilo Bambang Yudhoyono would regard with insouciance my Bushido, my bravado in corralling many of my favourite words into one single, glorious sentence. In fact, I think they would say that all of this was just tickety-boo.

The karma in taking the biscuit

Biscuit barrel rummaging is sneaky and unfair

I AM in a quandary. At one of the two workplaces I occasionally visit there is a biscuit barrel in the tearoom. Now, in an unusual display of management largesse, this barrel is replenished every morning with none other than Arnott's Family Assorted biscuits. You will be familiar with these biscuits. There's the dark Chocolate Ripple, the rich Scotch Finger, the cute Teddy Bear and the bland Milk Coffee and Milk Arrowroot. Ahh, but then there is the highly prized and the oh-so-nutty Butternut Snap. I'm not usually a biscuit person, but I must admit that when I skip breakfast I have been known to use the tongs provided to fish out a biscuit to accompany my morning tea. And for years when I have done this I have followed the unspoken Biscuit Barrel Protocol, which dictates that whomsoever should visit upon the biscuit barrel is obliged morally and philosophically to take a selection from whatever biscuits fate has delivered to the surface of the barrel. In short, it's bad form to rummage for a Butternut Snap when there's a Milk Coffee on top. And for years I have accepted my fate: I accepted I was simply unlucky when it came to the random selection of biscuits. Fate would never yield unto me a Scotch Finger let alone a Butternut Snap. And it never occurred to me to question the grand design of the biscuit barrel's biscuit allocation.

Then over Christmas I had a revelation of sorts. Can it be mere coincidence that whenever I go to the biscuit barrel all the good biscuits are gone? Surely God is not conspiring to float Butternut Snaps to the surface for others, but when he sees me heading for the tearoom he deliberately sinks those nutty Butternut Snaps to the barrel's bottom and beyond the convenient reach of my tongs? Upon deliberation I have concluded this is no coincidence and that God is probably not behind it. Do you know what I really think? I think there is a Biscuit Barrel Rummager who gets in early and who does over the barrel before anyone else gets a chance at the Butternut Snaps. I make two observations about this sad state of affairs. First, why has it taken years for this revelation to occur to me? Am I really so naive as to think that some people of questionable biscuit ethics wouldn't rummage a barrel in search of a better biscuit? And, second, how does this person (or persons—I wouldn't rule out a Biscuit Collaboration) live with themselves?

If you are the Biscuit Barrel Rummager at one of my two workplaces and you are reading this, I hope you feel guilty. And I hope that those unfairly gained Butternut Snaps have converted into kilos that will not budge from your hips, where they might serve as a permanent reminder of your ill-gotten gains. But most of all I hope that when you read this, Biscuit Barrel Rummager, you will mend your ways and join those of us who understand the importance of the Biscuit Barrel Protocol: sometimes you need to take what life dishes out and accept it.

Life isn't all Butternut Snap, you know. Sometimes you have to work your way through bland bits to get to the good bits.

Life's pleasures help you keep your shirt on

It's may be all gloom and doom but there is always a bright side

I DON'T know. Every night on television and every day in the papers it's one bad news story after another. Now I do get this: life can be tough. And yes, Greece is about to explode. Or is it the global economy that is set to collapse because of quantitative easing? Do you know I hadn't heard of the term *quantitative easing* until recently; apparently it means 'to print money' and it's yet another thing that's going to bring us undone. And yes, I do understand that we Australians in particular are going to be made redundant by new technology and by workers in Guangzhou who can produce twice as much for half the cost. It really is doom and gloom everywhere.

Yet every day I get up, as indeed do millions of others, and we go about our business as if nothing was wrong. It's almost as if we push to the back of our minds the political mess, the budgetary dilemmas, the petty politicking, the imminent global disasters that will surely befall us, all because we like to get by instead by thinking about life's small pleasures. The media may be full of imminent disaster but on a day-to-day basis I think most people are preoccupied with small pleasures and with equally small problems. Not that these pleasures and problems appear small to us.

For example, I get an inordinate amount of pleasure from getting my week's dry-cleaned business shirts every Saturday morning. Five shirts washed, ironed, lightly starched, folded and wrapped in plastic (for travel interstate) and delivered to my door for $29. How good is that? I mean how good is that? They're so crisp and clean and white and—yes I am going to say it—virginal; they're so delectable just waiting to be, well, you know, worn. Is it wrong that my mind is preoccupied with the minutiae of laundered shirts when the world's about to collapse? Or should I simply enjoy this moment as one of life's simple pleasures?

The same logic applies to problems. There are the big intractable problems that seem to consume the media; then there are the immediate problems that are in fact more likely to cause physiological distress. Not being able to find a parking space, for example. Or suffering through the company of an interminable bore at a work 'do'. Or finding an empty milk carton in the fridge because it, like, takes so much effort to, like, walk 2 metres to the recyclables bin.

It's almost as if there's a hierarchy of concerns that occupy our waking moments. There are the serious concerns that consume media attention, but effectively these matters have little bearing on how we conduct our daily life. In fact our minds are much more likely to be preoccupied with the petty, the practical and/or indeed the unashamedly ephemeral stuff of life that litters our everyday existence. I am struggling with this dilemma. It's the big stuff that I think we are meant to be talking about, but it's the small stuff that in many ways has a bearing on human contentment. Perhaps there needs to be a recalibration. Life is a pastiche of the big and the small, of the near and the far of problems and of pleasures. And if this is the case, then there needs to be a legitimisation of the thought processes that go into what might be called 'sweating the small stuff'. Okay, so I'm probably not going to solve the Greek debt crisis with this comment, but in this moment and in this place this issue is important to me.

So would you please not put empty milk cartons back in the fridge door for someone else to transfer to the recyclables bin? And why can't all shopping centres have a system to show the location of available parking spaces? Surely it's not wrong for me to get excited about the quality, the value, the unashamed easiness of it all in opening my laundered, folded, virginal packaged shirts on a Saturday morning while you're reading this column.

Supermarket of dreams

Strategies for getting through the checkout

I HAVE a confession. I know what I am about to say might shock some people but it's also the truth. I have a passion that no one knows about. Until now, that is.

I like supermarkets. I like big supermarkets. I like big supermarkets where the shopping is easy and the parking is plentiful. I like big supermarkets with big trolleys that are light and new and where the grip thing is clean and the wheels swivel in any direction. When I pull trolleys out, I discretely give them a bit of a swivel test to ensure that I get one that manoeuvres easily and responsively. If I am in an aisle and I have to move quickly to avoid an awkward Trolley Bump Incident with another shopper, I like to

know that my wheels will respond as directed. I like supermarkets where there are lots of staff with brightly coloured
vests so that I can ask where the coconut milk is 'because I
looked in the Asian section and it's not there'.

'Oh, it is there.'

'Sorry.'

'Thank you.'

I even like supermarket music. It makes me feel happy.
It's February and I'm still humming 'Winter Wonderland':
'Something, something, something … walking in a winter
wonderland.' What's not to like about that?

At my local supermarket there are ten parking spaces
between the store door and the trolley return. Not only are
these spots strategically positioned but they are on the high
side of a sloping car park. Runaway trolleys don't bang into
cars parked on the high side. I feel like a winner when I get
that one of those parks.

I also like it when I walk into the supermarket and I see
twenty checkouts and fifteen are open and there are barely
one or two shoppers at each checkout. One or two shoppers at each checkout! Yes. I have seen this. Some checkout
operators are standing, chatting with each other; they are
in an idling situation just waiting for me to appear with
my laden trolley. They could do me straight away if I was
ready. Straight away! Can you imagine?

But my initial excitement over a no-queue checkouts
situation quickly gives way to anxiety. Deep inside I know
this situation is unsustainable; it is too good to last. It's only
a matter of time before supermarket management spots the
inefficiency and sends some operators home. Suddenly my
supermarket visit turns into a race against the clock. If I do
this aisle and that aisle, focusing on the essentials first and

the nice-to-haves later, and if I keep doubling back to the checkout end, I can monitor the Average Queue Length of the checkout bank at five-minute intervals. If there should be a material change to the queue situation, I think that after fifteen minutes I could pull into the closest low-queue checkout.

And as I smugly leave that checkout with my neatly bagged groceries having waited no time at all, I will look over at the checkout supervisor on her platform behind the cigarette counter and I'll give her my best I-beat-the-system look. And she'll glare back slightly miffed but haughty with her we'll-get-you-next-time look. And then I'll push my big, true-wheeled trolley barely 25 metres to my car and then I'll walk that empty trolley barely 7 metres to the trolley-return thing. And don't you go thinking I've made up those distances.

And that is why I like supermarkets. Supermarket shopping isn't about food provisioning; it's a game of strategy and chance where only the audacious might dare to beat the system. Ha ha ha.

Bernard is just so last century

Some names just aren't meant to stick

I WANT to talk about given or Christian names. For more than fifty years I have had daily experience interacting with others, responding to, projecting and spelling my name, and generally being labelled as a complete 'Bernard'. And for much of that time, let me assure you, that Bernard was pretty much Bernard. Nothing fancy, schmancy or even racy; Bernard was, well, Bernard. In fact, the only other Bernards I knew came from my Catholic primary school, where a bunch of Bernards ruled the playground along with a block of Brendans, a gaggle of Gerards and a cacophony of Kevins. Bernard is a time capsule from the late 1950s and 60s; by the 1970s, the name had fallen out of common usage, even among the most devout Catholics. So for much of my youth, outside the primary school cocoon, I rarely came across another Bernard, and especially not in business. Business names that I came across were more likely to be Andrew, Richard or John. For some reason the Bernard genus never flourished in business.

In fact, I am mightily suspicious. Exactly where have all the Bernards gone? Has there been a Bernard ethnic cleansing that I am unaware of? Oh, there are a few us Bernards who have managed to survive into the twenty-first century, but we are a rare breed. There are the musician Bernard Fanning and the tennis player Bernard Tomic, not to mention a particularly droll Bernard from *Yes, Minister*. But I cannot name another Bernard, and yet there were so many all those years ago. Once upon a time the Bernards roamed free and wild, but now they cling to life wherever they can get a foothold: music here, tennis there, even 'demographics' can sustain life for these desperate creatures. Even if all the Bernards alive today were rounded up and put into a protected habitat, I still doubt there would be any left by the middle of the century.

You do realise that there is a Secret Society of Bernards. Oh, yes. We have a secret handshake that I could not possibly divulge. Here's how the society works. Whenever one

Bernard is introduced to another Bernard, be it in business or socially, do you know what we do? We mentally take note of each other. That's right. We think: Hmm, another Bernard. Interesting. I could name pretty much every Bernard I have met in business during the past twenty years. There are fewer than six. Six! You can't continue a life form with six specimens. Something needs to be done. And quickly, lest this nation be completely Bernard-less by 2050.

Ahh, but it's not just the mysterious disappearance of 1960s Bernards that I fear; it is the rebranding of those Bernards that do survive. Consider the evidence. The name Bernard when expressed in its original playground form was delivered as a single (admittedly mangled) syllable, as in 'bernrd'. Not so today. My 22-year-old daughter's generation Y friends have trouble pronouncing Bernard. They insist on giving it a cosmopolitan affectation with two syllables, as in Ber-Nard. The Secret Society of Bernards rejects this pronunciation as being too posh.

Bernard, along with Brendan, Gerard and Kevin, are all relics from another era, along with other Catholic relics like Maureen. Apparently the devout named their children after a saint, and since there are no Saints Brock, Finn or Kyle, the regular saints, such as Bernard, were frequently called upon to give up their names to new babies. It has to be said that plain-Jane Bernard is not a particularly creative name, and yet it barely survived a decade beyond popularity. I suspect that many of today's especially creative Christian names will be fortunate to survive the decade. In fact, there may well be a Secret Society of Brocks in the 2020s whose aim it will be to promote the interests of middle-aged paunchy men called Brock.

Detritus is us, like it or not

Why can't we bring ourselves to dump junk?

WHEN I go on holiday I tend to stay not in hotels but in apartments. You get so much more space. And you can get your own breakfast at a fraction of the cost. I am at heart a frugal person; post-tax money is hard enough to come by without wasting it, I say. But frugality is not my point; my point is how confronting it is to stay in a rented apartment. This is like a mini-me home: everything you need to sustain life is in that apartment. Even cooking utensils. Open the drawer near the sink and there is a cutlery set all laid out with forks, knives and spoons in separate compartments. Please note: there's no reckless cutlery crossover in rented apartments. I get a tiny frisson of pleasure whenever I see such order. Sigh. In another drawer there will be a carving knife, a vegetable peeler, a can opener and a spatula. Not two spatulas but one. And that's because you only need one spatula to spatulise whatever it is that you are cooking. Can you believe that all you need to live a comfortable life is contained within a rented apartment?

Then I go home and the comparisons start. There is a drawer in my kitchen that is difficult to shut because it's crammed with cooking utensils. Three wooden spoons at last count, one of which has a broken handle—but hey, why buy a new one, given they cost $1.85 each? Five cork-screw bottle openers (and I don't drink). Three egg rings (one of which is square). And much, much more. I have never used an egg ring. No one in my household has used an egg ring. How did three technically virginal egg rings find their way into my kitchen drawer? Is this part of an alien conspiracy to infiltrate households with egg ring–like beings that will spring into life at a given moment?

Then it struck me. I suspect as much as 20 per cent of stuff in middle-class households is probably not necessary; it's the detritus build-up of a consumer culture. This led me to some dangerous thinking. How many ties do I own? I am embarrassed to say more than fifty. How many ties do I currently wear? Perhaps five. At best. Oh please, give me a break; some of these ties go back to when I started work. One has polka dots. Not cute, discreet little dots but big, bold, in-your-face polka dots. One day I am going to wake up and big, bold polka dots will be back in fashion and I will breeze over to my tie rack, shake that polka dot tie out of its hibernation and glide off to work with an air of frugal smugness. Tsk tsk, every other male must buy his big, bold polka dot tie but I just had to dip into my tie collection.

But there's a problem. Do I space all my ties equally on a tie rack or should I put some into cryogenic suspension? Is it fair for three never-used egg rings to claim real estate in a utensils drawer when realistically their chances of being used are less than once in a decade? Now, I know what you're thinking. Why not throw some stuff out or give it to the Salvos? But a lot of stuff is not good enough to use, yet is too good to throw out or too sentimentally precious to give away. Have you ever held on to something from your youth, say a tie, and then discarded it in a Brotherhood bin? Do you hear a pathetic cry of abandonment as that innocent tie falls helplessly into the darkness of a cold steel bin? Sure, it will go to a good home. But will it be loved as it deserves to be loved?

Perhaps that's why we hang on to such things: they connect us to previous lives, times and relationships. And so the unfashionable ties and the virginal egg rings sit proudly but silently, patiently, resolutely, amid the hurly burly of everyday life, awaiting the glorious day of their resurrection into common use. Or indeed perhaps awaiting that other terrible day of judgment when, in a frenzied determination to streamline our lives, we casually dispatch such detritus to another place for eternity.

Beds tart up to go front of house

There's plenty of action in baby boomer bedrooms ... on the bed

SOMETHING odd is happening inside the Australian home. The furniture is on the move. There was a time when beds lived in the bedroom and couches lived in the lounge room. But recently there has been a fusion, an unholy coming together if you like, of the bed and the couch. Gone are the two- and three-seater; in has come a new configuration that has plonked itself slap-bang in front of the plasma telly. This new thing is, I swear, half-couch, half-bed. Do you sit on it or do you sleep in it? The answer is neither. You and one other can sprawl all over it; not together—that would never do in a communal space—but at right angles, which is a good idea because while the heads can converse, the vital bits are pointing in divergent directions.

In the bedroom quite the reverse has happened: the plain-Jane bed has morphed into a work of fabric art. Once upon a time, beds were used for sleeping and were hidden from public view, but modern beds know that they are on show, especially those show-pony king-sized beds. Exactly how or why this has occurred is something of a mystery.

Why would anyone want to show anyone their bed? Okay, so some people may show some people their bed, but surely not every visitor to the house?

I suspect that beds started to get big ideas about, let's be frank, their prettiness when the design of houses changed. About twenty years ago the master bedroom migrated back to the front of the house and, with bedroom door completely akimbo, or even teasingly ajar, a bold bed vista is afforded to any visitor who may walk down the hall. Of course, as soon as the bed knew that it was being watched, do you know what that cheap hussy of a piece of furniture did? That's right: it started tarting itself up. Some pieces of furniture have no shame. Long gone is the shapeless bedspread; in has come a series of scatter cushions and pillows as well as something I have yet to work out the purpose of: it goes by the name of a throw and I suspect it may even possess an exotic spelling.

The bed is at the epicentre of what can only be described as the pillowfication of the bedroom. Pillows and cushions have crystallised on the bed and they are multiplying. The pillowfication process gives an otherwise flat bed curves. The modern bed is on display for all to see, and this piece of furniture is lovin' the attention. 'Look at me. Look at me. I'm a bed and I'm all covered in pillows. Perhaps you'd like to, ahem, tuck me in?' Ahh, but before you yield to a pillowfied bed's comely delights you should understand that these pillows are not for messing with. No, no, no. These pillows are for looking at. Did you realise that these pillows are never just scattered; even though one goes by the name of 'scatter cushion', they are laid out to a grand and secret design. Square cushions, for example, cannot be laid square with the bed; they must be set on the diagonal so as to please the eye. Did your eye know that it was displeased with square-set pillows? No, neither did mine, but apparently it was mightily offended. I think it's time for a bedroom intervention before the show-pony king-sized bed drowns in pillows, cushions and throws.

In praise of the foreign phrase

Words commandeered from other languages make all the difference to English

I AM an aficionado, a devotee, an apparatchik of the foreign phrase. I am also a sucker for a foreign accent. I like Irish, Scottish, cultivated Londoner (I could have listened to Princes Diana for hours) as well as all dialects and colonial incarnations of French, Spanish and Italian. I'm sure I would like Portuguese too but I've been to neither Lisbon nor Rio de Janeiro. Are all of these languages somehow linguistically connected or is it just that there is an inherent lilt and a poetic meter to their aural phrasing that I find inherently pleasing?

Now before you go all Latin-based romantic languages on me, I am also partial to softly spoken, not to mention quietly sung, German. I can't wait till I am next sitting in Vienna's Café Sperl and am asked what song I'd like to hear next because I'm going to say in my best German accent, '"Eine kleine Nachtmusik", *s'il vous plait*.' And if that doesn't impress the locals, I'll ask for the oh-so-dreamy 'Stille Nacht'. No. No. Wait. I have it. Is there anything more moving than the brave widower Georg von Trapp singing 'Edelweiss', *sotto voce*, to his captivated children with just a hint of an Austrian accent? So manly. So gentle. So alone. He just needs to be loved. Mind you, the Germans have also given us *blitzkrieg* from war and the bizarre *schadenfreude*, meaning 'to take pleasure in the misfortunes of others'. That there was no word in the English language to adequately convey the concept behind *schadenfreude* is perhaps a credit to the English. Of course the German *schadenfreude* should not to be confused with the French *sang-froid*, which means 'coolness in trying circumstances'. And which is different to *savoir-faire*, again from the French, meaning 'to know exactly what to do in any situation, trying or not'. I quite like *suave* from the French, meaning 'smoothly polite', but this must never be confused with *soave*, which is a dry white wine from Italy's Veneto region.

There are even some pronunciations of the New York accent that I find irresistible, especially the 'o' sound. Jerry Seinfeld, for example, has a most engaging 'o' pronunciation. He says *go* and *show* with a deliciously rounded 'o'. I wish I could say *go* and *show* like Jerry but unfortunately my articulations of these words are all too short, flat and stumpy. Whenever I am in the US I am often asked if I'm from London. They know I'm not a local and that I speak English, so the only other non-American English-speaking place I could possibly come from is London, England, right?

Have you ever wondered why certain foreign words were absorbed into the English language and why they are still used today? *Bushido*, *bravado* and *chutzpah* all mean pretty much the same thing, but obviously they have had to be imported from the Japanese, the Spanish and the Yiddish because nothing quite like these terms existed locally. The Anglosphere does not know bravado, but the

Spanish clearly do, so they said, 'Here you go, amigos; you can borrow our term.'

But I think it's the French who have most effectively infiltrated the English language, *n'est-ce pas*? Nothing adds piquancy, that certain *je ne sais quois*, to a thought in the English world than a brief foray, a short sortie, into the French. And yet the irony is that it is the French who have resisted a reciprocal English invasion through the moderating efforts of the *patriotique* Académie française. The French have given the English-speaking world words to show light and shade, as in, for example, *fiance* and *fiancée*. In the blunt Anglo world, the only term required was *betrothed*, and it applied equally to all parties intended for marriage. But for some reason, the French needed to know who was betrothed. Was it the male or was it the female? Why they would need to make this distinction is unclear, but it is this very specificity that makes many French and other foreign words so right in so many English-speaking contexts. But then perhaps that is why English has been such a successful language. It is absorbant; it is adaptable; and it is accurate: if nothing exists locally, we cheerily scan the globe to find exactly the right word to describe our needs and our observations.

Lured to the dark side

Transferring from tea to coffee

YOU might recall a piece I wrote in this column just over a year ago where I lamented the fact that tea drinkers such as me are treated like second-class citizens when it comes to beverage matters. Coffee people get groovy baristas who steamily inscribe pagan designs in the froth of a flat white. And they do this for no other reason than to please the eye of a coffee drinker. What do tea drinkers get from a barista, apart from a sneer? We get a tea bag and a cup of not-nearly-hot-enough water. And that is it. Tea people have been conditioned to expect less than coffee people. I clearly touched a nerve with my tea *cri de cœur*. Tea drinkers the country over rose up as one and issued a very stern tut-tut to the entire coffee nation. We sure showed those coffee drinkers a thing or two.

But despite or perhaps because of my background as a Tea Activist, I have done something I now need to get off my chest. After a lifetime of tea drinking, and I have to say of moaning about coffee people, I have … I have … I have crossed over to the other side. From the tea side to the coffee side. I know, I know. Look, it all happened so quickly.

I was in Havana, Cuba last November. I was on holiday. It was hot. It was steamy. You know how addled my brain gets when it's steamy. I asked for tea. I wanted tea. My body was expecting tea. But they don't do tea in Cuba. They do coffee. They do seductive coffee. They do temptress coffee. They do drink-me-now coffee. I didn't go looking for coffee. Coffee came looking for me. Oh get thee behind me thou wicked, wanton, wily coffee. Ye shall tempt me not from my tea. Thine silky, dark, aromatic guile shall pass not my lips. Well, it was late. There was rhythmic music pulsing through the heavy Havana air. The end of the meal came and there was an expectant pause.

'*Café, señor?*' Where there was usually tea there was suddenly coffee. Indeed there was oh-so-drinkable coffee. And

I have to say that in a single moment of weakness, I crossed the Beverage Line from pure black tea to flat white coffee.

'*Si, café. Por favor.*' And *si, si, si*, I have to say that I enjoyed it. I really enjoyed it. Of course it was over in a few minutes but such was the sensation that I knew I had to have more. Oh I'm not saying that I am now crazily drinking instant coffee in a polystyrene cup (although I have clearly thought about it); what I am saying is that my intrinsic beverage compass has shifted. Ever since that moment I have been ordering flat white coffees in smart cafés in Sydney and Melbourne much to the astonishment of companions who, I have to say, have known and endured for years the full force of my righteous tea rigidity.

But here's the thing. Late at night at home while watching the telly I don't have a hankering for coffee; I have a desire for tea. Simple, clean, hot, pure, sugarless tea. Served in a translucent fine-china cup and saucer. I drink tea in private but now I drink coffee in public. I have discovered that I am bi-drinkual and I no longer care who knows. *Viva café. Gracias Havana.*

5

Generations and Ageing

SOME people think that too much time and too much brain space are allocated to the issue of generational behaviour. I'm not one of those people. I am, and I know many others are also, endlessly fascinated with the concept of generational transition. I also suspect that this fascination grows with age. Up to the mid forties not much attention is paid to the issue of 'the youth of today' since 'the youth of today' that relates to adults under the age of forty-five generally comprises children. By the fifties, however, a different perspective emerges: the young people dealt with by that age—at work and at home—tend to be twenty-something and have formulated their own responses to issues such as work and relationships. By this time in the life cycle, comparisons can be made between the way different generations have addressed the issue of, say, courtship or work or familial relationships. There's also much time spent by parents wondering about their children: their wellbeing, their prospects, their relationships, their special talents and why these qualities aren't being duly recognised by others. Again, it is not so much whether these ruminations are right or wrong or fair or unfair; the point is that the issue of generations and ageing dominates a lot of what people think about on a day-to-day basis.

Trapped in life's sandwich

Some people are being squeezed at both ends … so to speak

I WANT to talk to you about a brand new generation that has only recently been discovered. I want to talk about the sandwich generation. This refers to people, usually in their fifties, who—if you will excuse the unfortunate imagery—are being squeezed at both ends. They are sandwiched between their amazing twenty-something, generation-Y children and their frail eighty-something parents. And the reason why the sandwichers—or should that be sandwichistas?—are so new is that, first, previous generations of twenty-somethings left the family home as soon as they could. (I mean—let's be frank—if you wanted to sleep with your girlfriend in the 1970s, this was never going to happen in the family home. Officially. Apparently.) And, second, previous generations of fifty-somethings did not have parents to care for. Parents used to conveniently drop dead long before they wandered into that part of the life cycle when they required care. And so it was that the sandwich generation came into being soon after the turn of the twenty-first century.

One part of the sandwich—the twenty-something stay-at-home kids—has been buttering-up Mum and Dad for the better part of a decade. What has emerged this decade is the other side of the sandwich: the crusty but piquant parental topping. Gen Ys are fun to manage for fifty-somethings: you get to moan about this lot not leaving home, but the reality is that having them around makes the middle-aged feel needed. But the elderly-parents thing is a tough gig. You can't moan about caring for the old the way you can about the young. At least not directly. Better to be discreet and tell all and sundry how busy you are. Busy looking after others, that's you. That's life inside the sandwich.

Do you know what most upsets the sandwichers? It's not the time; it's not the emotion; it's not the opportunity cost of giving up work to care for others; it's not even the relentlessness of it all; it's what I like to call 'the spread'. This is the idea that the responsibility for looking after Mum and Dad falls by default to the son or daughter who happens to be living in closest proximity. Siblings who long ago left the parental home, suburb, town or country can happily absolve themselves of all responsibility and leave it to their local familial counterparts. 'Look, I'd love to visit Mum and Dad more often but as you know I have a very important job poncing around with very important people here in London—or is that New York, or perhaps Sydney?—so I guess you'll have to do it all. Ciao.'

Ciao? Ciao? I'll ciao you, you … oh, never mind.

And if the local familial counterpart happens to be a son, the parental-care thing often falls to a daughter-in-law. It's odd, don't you think, that the final years of a long life can be spent in the company of the woman who marries your son?

And then there's the behaviour that really infuriates sand-wichers: guilt-ridden, London-living, highfalutin sibling flies in once a year, makes a lot of noise, tells everyone what to do, complains about 'what needs to happen' and then returns from whence they came, superficially content in the knowl-edge that they have 'fixed the Mum and Dad issue'. Do you know why this so infuriates sandwichers? It's not because these once-a-year blowhards blow in and blow out; it's because the gentle sandwichers can't quite bring themselves to have it out and create a fuss. And, besides, it'd upset Mum and Dad. That's why sandwichers are sandwichers: they give where others cannot—or simply will not—give. That's the sandwichers' strength as well as their weakness. They pick up the slack, enabling others not to pull their weight. I think there's a sandwicher in most modern families.

Now if you'll excuse me, I have some very important things to do with some very important people. Would you mind cleaning up? Ciao.

Averting an X-rated explosion

Let's talk about the forgotten generation

I DO so like generation X. That they are a handsome race is neither in dispute nor the basis of my admiration. The reason I like generation X is because they are such good sports. They don't complain and yet they have every right to. Here they are now, aged 34–49, falling slap-bang in the middle of the difficult years of child-rearing and career development, and what do we hear from them? Nuthin'. Not a peep. Not a sausage. Xers are either strong and silent types by nature or they are being drowned out by their noisy neighbours, the brash old baby boomers and the blunt young generation Y.

Now, when boomers were having kids and building careers in the 1980s, all we ever heard about was Dinks (double income, no kids) and Yuppies (young upwardly mobile professionals). And when generation Y entered the workforce last decade, all we ever heard about was how talented and special they were. Are. So sorry, generation Y. My mistake. It was a mouth malfunction. Are special.

Phew, that was close. I implied that generation Y was not currently special. I think I got away with it.

You do realise that I claim to be a generation Xer. Oh yes, it's just that I am trapped in a hideous baby-boomer body. I especially admire generation X mothers. I like their attitude to parenting: Look kid, I work; get over it; you're not special; that's the way it is. Now clean up your room! Hands up those who like to see children being disciplined in public by parents? And by disciplined I don't mean in a politically incorrect, corporal-punishment sort of way, but in a firm, show-the-child-boundaries sort of way. I go weak at the knees whenever I see these rare acts performed in public. I want to walk up to the parent—male or female— and say something uncharacteristically American like 'You go, girl' or 'You go, bro'. This is so out of character for me, since I would never comment in the first place, and if I did I would not deploy a gauche American cliché. My gauche clichés are usually proudly Australian. And yet that's the response I feel whenever I see applied public parenting. It seems to me that no one steps out of line in generation Xer households, least of all children and husbands. And really, is there that much difference?

And there's a very good reason for this level of hyper-organisation in Xer homes: it's the only way a modern traditional nuclear family, with two full-time working parents, can make it work. Everyone must do their bit. There ain't no room for princesses in such a household. Boomers got fee-free tertiary education, relatively afford-able housing, and a boom economy when they peaked in their management careers. Generation Ys were fawned over by desperate employers in the mid-2000s. Xers had to pay for tertiary education through HECS; they copped higher housing costs, probably brought on by the boomer escalation of demand for housing; as graduates in the workplace, they had to kowtow to the established boomer hierarchy; and they didn't really get their hands on the top jobs until boomers deftly moved aside in the tough years following the global financial crisis. And yet Xers still don't complain about the unfairness of it all.

But I think that all this holding back of the need to tell it like it is is unnatural. Accordingly it is with great confidence that I predict a generational explosion at some point over the next decade when Xers suddenly share their innermost thoughts. Every resentment that Xers have ever felt—have ever stilled—will find voice as they cruise confidently to the peak of their careers. Empowered by success and enraged at past injustices, Xers are a powder keg that is bound to explode.

For the safety of all, may I suggest an intervention? Xers must be encouraged to let it out now, bit by bit, so as to avert a more calamitous explosion later in the decade. So, generation X, do you feel a tad left out? Are you sick of the boomers? And tell me how you feel about those pesky generation Ys? Let it out, Xers. Let it out. You'll feel so much better after you have let it all go.

Pity the poor parents

Adult children love to keep tabs on the whereabouts of Mum and Dad

THERE comes a time when the roles of parents and children reverse. The parent stops worrying about the child and the child starts worrying about the parent. I suspect that time is when children approach their quarter-life crisis: they hit twenty-five and question whether it's all downhill from here on. And as they look down from the heady heights of the lean and fit mid-twenties, they see ageing, flailing parents with dicky knees and dodgy hips, wallowing, unable to extricate themselves from the sticky mire of a fifty-something bog. And they take pity on parents as a consequence. They think, Poor, poor parents; it won't be long before we have to put them down.

The evidence for this sad state of affairs is plain for all to see. The said parents might be out. At night. In the dark. Doing who knows what with who knows whom. Eventually—maybe 9 pm—there is a call from an agitated child to the wayward parent.

'Where are you?'

'Who are you with?'

'When are you coming home?'

'Is there anything to eat in the fridge?'

When the child asks the parent, 'Where are you?' what they really mean to say is: 'I didn't think you went out at night? Don't you go to bed at, like, 9.30 or something? Sheesh. Disgusting.' Not that they say that, but I am sure that's exactly what they are thinking.

And when the child asks, 'Who are you with?' what they really mean to say is: 'I didn't think you had any, you know, like, friends. Like, I know you know people and stuff and you speak to people, but friends? Night friends? What do you do with these night friends? Nothing embarrassing I hope.' Again, not that they verbalise this, but I am sure from their tone and from the bits they leave unsaid that this is exactly what they mean.

And when the child asks, 'When are you coming home?' what they really mean to say is: 'I don't approve of you being out at night with people I don't know and for an indeterminate amount of time. Anything could happen to you. I have been worried sick.' And yet again they never actually say this, but they are thinking exactly this.

Then, of course, comes the clincher: when the child asks, 'Is there anything to eat in the fridge?' what they really mean to say is, 'I still need you', and that is the sweetest question of all.

But role reversal goes beyond concern for parents who may be up till the wee hours of 9 pm. At airports, at sporting and cultural events or at a social function such as a family wedding, the adult child is likely to be mindful of parents standing for way too long. 'Dad, why don't you sit here while I queue for the tickets?' And the reason why this arrangement is suggested is because they don't think you are up to standing for any length of time. They think that you are so old that you need their help. But they cannot say this, so role reversal happens around you and to you whether you like it or not.

Now I do get this: at some point in the continuum of life it is necessary for one life form to recede and die and for another to rise and bloom. But at what point does this transition take place? I think that a reasonable time for this to occur is the mid to late sixties. But with the advent of what I like to call role reversal syndrome, the parent gets no say in the matter. The child looks you up and down and comes to the conclusion that you need help with, you know, stuff. Initially the parent thinks, You beauty, all those years of teaching consideration for others is finally paying off. Then you realise what's going on, but by this time it's too late: the roles have begun their reversal. What we need is a protocol: an agreed arrangement that children should not pity their parents until late middle age. Or, if role reversal syndrome should apply from fifty onwards, then children are obligated to do a far better job of pretending that they are merely being considerate.

A generation misled by the great lie

Pandering to generation Y not such a good idea

WHEN US Secretary of State Hillary Clinton visited Melbourne in 2010, a youth forum was held where she prefaced her answers with comments such as 'That's a great question' and 'That's another terrific question'. So now generation Y gets validation for simply asking a question? Is this what we've come to? The same logic applies with Twitter feeds that scroll across the television during ABC1's *Q&A*: 'Great question.' And here I was thinking that the matter for judgment was the quality of the answer, not the alleged insight of the question.

Surely generation Y must find this patronising: is this a stalling tactic to create time to formulate an answer or is it a way of verbally patting a young questioner on the head for being so terribly clever? Either way, shouldn't the response be a polite 'Thank you, but could you answer the question?' But this is not the response. The questioner seems only too willing to accept accolades. And the reason generation Y responds this way is because its members have been inculcated from an early age with the notion that they are special. I suspect they have been reared in such a cocoon of undeserved praise that being congratulated for asking a question doesn't appear odd at all. And I don't necessarily limit this delusion of specialness to generation Y. I think it applies to many people born in the second half of the twentieth century. Perhaps this is a feature of small families with working parents; it gives rise to what the Chinese call little emperor syndrome. So much money, so few kids; they're so special. And so gorgeous. Yes, you are. Oh yes you are.

When I was a kid in the 1960s and we played pass the parcel, I quickly worked out that the game was rigged so the birthday boy always got the present. Today it's a different story. There's a present under every wrapper. No kid has to learn how to sit back and watch someone else win.

Look at Twitter profiles. Apparently it is not possible to define a tweeter with a single term. It requires a collection of tags: 'Father, husband, brother, lover of social media, occasional surfer, red-wine connoisseur'. And this is one of the worthier profiles I have come across. Excuse me, Twitter person, but no one cares. At least Twitter is mercifully brief. Facebook profiles can extend across pages that document the minutiae of, let's face it, ordinary lives. I didn't know your favourite colour was blue. That's brilliant. Do tell me more. What are the names of your pets? Oh, what a fascinating person you are. Actually, this is not fascinating; it's boring. What is fascinating is the presumption that anyone would think they are so fascinating that other people would want to know this detail about who they really are. Have you confused yourself with a celebrity? Do you think you are the next Brad Pitt or Angelina Jolie just waiting to be discovered? And that if you fill out this profile in jaunty

detail, including your many likes and dislikes, you may be
discovered and rescued from suburban life?

Having witnessed the rise of the specialness delusion, I
am concerned about the future of generation Y. At some
point down the track many young people will come to
the sad realisation that they have been lied to all their
lives. What Mum and Dad said, what teachers said, what
friends said, what fawning employers said, was all wrong:
you are not amazing; at best you have a modest talent in
a limited field. In fact, no one ever read any more than
the first line of your Facebook profile. And that blog you
ran—that was going to make you the blogger-made-good
Perez Hilton of the environmental world—was only read
by your friends, and even they skimmed it. The danger that
flows from an outbreak of specialness delusion is that it is
inevitably followed by a dose of middle-age reality. Perhaps
generation Y will eventually be known not for the flighti-
ness of their youth but for their disappointment later in
life. Ultimately, generation Y could be known as the disap-
pointed generation.

The dye is cast as middle age approaches

At least some middle-aged men have hair to dye

THERE comes a point in every man's life when he starts to
notice other men's hair. And it's not just whether he's got
any or not; it's also about the colour. Is it just me moving
yet further into middle age, or are baby-boomer men
increasingly dyeing their hair? There I am in a business
meeting with another fifty-something male and while he

is speaking all I can think of is, Have you dyed your hair? Not that I verbalise this thought, but I am thinking it. And do you know, there comes a point in the meeting when I reckon that the hair-dye guy knows that I am on to his hair-dyeing ways. Not that there's anything wrong with men dyeing their hair. I suppose this is nothing more than yet another sign of the transition into middle age: that he would dye his hair and that I would notice.

Which brings me to my point. At what time in life do you stop being young and start being middle-aged? In 1968 John Lennon, at the age of twenty-eight, reportedly said, 'Don't trust anyone over thirty.' He thought middle age started at thirty, four decades ago. Tour operator Contiki limits its 'young' tours to 18–35-year olds, which means that, technically, you can be thirty-five years and eleven months and still hang out with eighteen-year-olds. Whether you would want to is not the point. The point is that by Contiki's measure, middle age starts at thirty-six. Homer Simpson, I am reliably informed, is thirty-seven and has remained so ever since his creator, Matt Groening, launched him in 1987. Personally I have always thought Homer looks more fifties than thirties. But perhaps this was the view of middle age in the 1980s: married men with children looked middle aged by their late thirties. I suspect if Homer was created today he would be placed in his late forties.

Get out your family photograph album and look at pictures of your grandparents at the age of fifty. They looked old; they dressed old; they behaved old. And with life expectancy before World War II extending only to sixty-five, by your mid-fifties you were entitled to look old because you were a decade from death. Not like today. At fifty you think that you have another thirty years of healthy, active life.

The old adage about life extending for 'three score and ten' years has blown out with baby-boomer expectations of four score and more.

I think there should be a rule that you are not allowed to act old until you are in the final 10 per cent of life. Based on today's life span this means that middle age should extend to seventy-four, which is 90 per cent of the average life span of eighty-two. But this doesn't answer my question about the year at which middle age begins. The philosophical views on the subject offered by Lennon, Groening and Contiki are dated. If life expectancy is eighty-two, then the midpoint is forty-one. Perhaps this is middle age, then.

But if you take an existential view (you can see that I am quite obsessed with this subject), then middle age should exist as an independent state within adult life. And since adult life is said to begin at twenty-one, this means the halfway point is fifty-one. And this is, oddly enough, precisely the age at which I first started noticing other men's hair. Ergo, modern middle age starts at fifty-one and lasts until seventy-four after which you have permission to act old.

Although I must say these dates are not necessarily fixed: generation Y insists on postponing commitment, which suggests the start to adult life is being delayed. And advances in medicine mean life expectancy will soon pass beyond the mid-eighties. By means of fancy figure work and at times contorted philosophical logic, I can argue the case that middle age doesn't start until fifty. And further that middle age is a moving target headed for sixty. But even if my case for the advancement of middle age is completely delusional, I know that there's a big market of hair-dyeing baby boomers who connect exactly with my train of thought.

The empty nesters' trump cards

No kidding, eligible baby boomers love this parlour game

THERE is a game that is played by baby boomer parents throughout Australia. The game is called My Kids Are Overseas, Where Are Yours? This is a parlour game that requires no fewer than three, but preferably four or more players. Here's how it works. Players should be aged fifty or over; they need to be old enough to have twenty-something kids. More often than not players are drawn from the professional, urban middle class and are therefore quite predisposed to overseas travel. The reason you need at least three is that the talker needs listeners for the game to work.

The scene is a social gathering of baby boomers. The chat quickly turns to children when someone opens the batting. 'Well, I simply must tell you all that Andrew and Fiona have arrived in London and are having an absolute wow of a time. Doing all sorts of exciting things. Popping over to Paris at the weekend.' Nicely pitched. Straight bat. Went with the classic London–Paris opener, which is always a favourite with baby-boomer parents.

The idea is for parents to one-up other parents with the ever more exciting and cosmopolitan locations that their generation-Y children are living or working in. Speak to the ruling elite of any country town in Australia, not to mention the upper middle class in a city such as Adelaide or Auckland or even Melbourne or Sydney, and while they will extol the virtues of their city, you will find that their kids are often living anywhere but in that city.

Let's get back to the game. You would think it's hard for anyone to top a London–Paris story, but I've seen it done. 'Oh, how wonderful for them both. We do so adore London at this time of year, and as for Paris, well, it's always gorgeous. Did I tell you that Alistair and Amanda left last weekend? Oh yes. New York. Well, actually, they intend spending part of the year in New York and part in Milan. We're meeting them for Christmas at Villa d'Este on Lake Como.'

In this game the objective is to project your kids as being more exotic, more global, more successful, more engaged and living in more important overseas locations than the children of others in the group. So saying that your daughter is working in Auckland isn't really a competitive statement, is it? The same goes for Singapore, Jakarta, Bangkok and Hong Kong. All too close and all far too accessible. Points are awarded for distance from Australia: London, Paris and New York score most, although Berlin is making a surprising move up the points table.

Points are also awarded for engagement: merely travelling through an exotic and important city is not really good enough. Working for a London law firm is good. Working as a judge's assistant on a noteworthy case is better. Working in Wall Street is also good. Or at least it was until the global financial crisis, but I think sufficient time has passed now for the New York option to be reinstated. Working for a fashion house in Paris or Milan or, get this, Prenzlauer Berg in Berlin is better still.

No. No. Wait. I have it. 'My son is working for an ethically caring global finance house based in Wall Street which is financing a Paris-based fashion house showcasing in Milan, so he and his partner and their gorgeous two-year-old daughter Chloe (or Miffy or Maddy or Pippa) are forever flitting between JFK and CDG.'

And after having topped everyone else's stories about their kids in—scoff—Vancouver or Ulaanbaatar or Wellington, the best way to seal the victory is with a complaint—yes, a complaint—about the cosmopolitanism of your son's life-style and success. 'Oh yes. Well, it sounds all very glamorous flitting between New York and Paris, but poor Alistair—it's all terribly exhausting. I'm very worried about him. I said to him, "Alistair, why don't you come back to Australia?" And he said, "Mum, I'd love to. But there's nothing for me there."'

Perfecto. Nothing and no one can top this. You've got the world cities thing happening. You've got the commercial success. You've woven in some chichi French sophistication. You've got the exasperation of it all. And you've let everyone know that you've been so successful as a parent that you have catapulted your son out of this dreary colonial outpost and into a place that is really exciting and that really matters. Congratulations, baby-boomer parent—you have just won My Kids Are Overseas, Where Are Yours?

The Frugals' war against want

Perhaps the Frugals really are the original greenies

I HAVE a soft spot for the Frugals. Don't know the Frugals? These are elderly creatures who come from the dark side of the Great Depression. Now aged eighty and over, they reflect an Australia that is receding. We have fewer than 93 000 Frugals; their number is declining by 5000 a year.

The Frugals are an odd life form. They value bizarre concepts such as 'going without' and 'self-sacrifice'. They put up with situations rather than complain. Imagine that. Putting up with something rather than complaining to someone, anyone. How weird are these people? Not only that, but Frugals have their very own language. They turn on the wireless. They talk about New Australians. They refer to the lush greenery behind Cairns as the jungle. The jungle! The Daintree might have been a jungle when soldiers were being trained for the Kokoda Track but to anyone born after World War II this is a gentle rainforest. Soldiers inhabit jungles; fairies, leprechauns and Yuppies inhabit rainforests. The Frugals have very different lifestyles. They eat chops and vegies and for a treat they go to a local pub and have a slap-up counter meal. You can tell if it's a good counter meal because the steak's 'yea thick'. 'And you can go back to the salad bar as often as you like.' How good is that? Mind you, the Frugals don't go out much. Why go out to eat when you could buy a week's groceries for the price of a main course in a fancy-pants restaurant?

Not that the Frugals push their lifestyle on to others, but they do, amid their own, murmur quietly about the ways of modern youth. 'Modern youth' refers to all and sundry born after 1946. Yep, that includes baby boomers, Xers, Ys and now the Zeds. Not for Frugals the flashiness of 'fashion clothes'. Why would you want new clothes when your old ones haven't worn out? Apart from during the war, the Frugals haven't been outside Australia but they did 'tootle around' when they retired in the 1980s. 'Why would you want to go overseas when you haven't seen your own back yard?' (Frugals, and no other generation, 'tootle'; to tootle is to motor aimlessly around Australia.)

The Frugals, largely born in the 1920s, might be regarded as the Generation of the Damned. Not for anything they have done, but rather for their unfortunate timing in life. Over-85s remember the Great Depression, and after they got through that, what did fate deliver? A world war in which they either fought or lost husbands, brothers and lovers. Being born between the catastrophes of World War I and the Great Depression and having to fight in a war would shape your world view. And that's precisely what happened. Frugals believe in a God of some sorts. And it's not hard to see why. If this life is marred by war and depression, then surely the next life must be better. Not like today: why believe in the next life when this life's so damned good? (How do you think a Church of St Hedonist the Redeemer would go? I reckon I'm on to a winner.)

Frugals are the original greenies; they waste not, want not. Did you know that Frugals darn socks? Dear Gen Y, let me explain: to darn a sock is to mend a hole with a needle and woollen thread. Frugals don't throw stuff out; they repair it. Imagine that! I sometimes wonder what Frugals think about their baby-boomer progeny and their generation-Y grandchildren. Is there an immense sense of pride in their achievements or is there despair for the lifestyles of a generation of self-absorbed wastrels? I don't suppose we'll ever know because they don't complain. Imagine that.

'Special' kids put boomers off course

They fear their offspring may not be ready for the real world

STAND by, I have a new theory. I call it my Special Theory of Baby Boomer Remorse. Now I know what you're thinking; you're thinking, I bet he's going to bang on about how middle-aged baby boomers regret not doing things in their youth that their kids are doing. When boomers were in their twenties do you know what they did? They studied; they worked; they got married; they saved for a house; some even had children. Can you imagine that? Having children in your twenties! No, oddly, I'm not going to bang on about that.

My theory relates to a growing sense of remorse that I think is gripping the baby-boomer race. A lot might be presumed about the way boomers see the world, but the one thing that you can say is that this lot were raised by parents who had been shaped by the Great Depression and World War II. These were tough people who had been through tough times, and when they had kids in the 1950s and 60s they didn't muck around when it came to the business of child rearing. 'Look, kid, here's what you do; now get on with it or you'll get a clip around the ear.' And if parents didn't give their boomer kids a clip around the ear, then it might be a teacher because, well, teachers were always right. Parental logic was simple: 'Here's your position in society, kid, and don't think about getting all uppity. What, do you think you're special or somethin'?'

And so as boomers made their way through the parenting 80s, the career-developing 90s and the career-peaking 2000s, do you know what they did? They gave their generation-Y children the upbringing that they never got. After all, wasn't this a sign of good parenting: to be generous and forthcoming; to heap the largesse of a successful career on a fortunate few children or on an exceptionally fortunate only child? Almost every child from this era was special: many got a name with special spelling to reflect their special qualities. And so for many years there was no such thing as boomer remorse. In fact it was quite the opposite; there was boomer pride: look at how much I'm doing for my kids; that makes me a good parent. Do you know what middle-class boomers like most? They love nothing better than recounting to all and sundry how many times their kids have been overseas.

But there comes a point later in life when boomers stop thinking about how wonderful they have been at providing and start thinking about how well they have prepared their children for the real world. Maybe, just maybe, it wasn't the right thing to be so forthcoming and generous to their generation Y children. Maybe, just maybe, the real measure of parenting success was not the ability to provide and to give, but to connect and to train. 'Look, kid, life's tough. You have to learn about the value of money. You have to make your way in a world where people might not appreciate the special qualities that your family and friends say that you have.'

Maybe the thing boomers should really have given their kids was not at all material. Perhaps in a consumerist world the gift parents really should give their children is the gift of restraint. Teaching modern children that 'stuff' doesn't come easily is a hard lesson to impart, especially if the parents have come from a financially strapped household and through tough times. That is what I mean about Baby Boomer Remorse: it is the realisation that boomers as parents might have been too materialistically generous to their kids. And indeed to such an extent that now they're concerned about how their children will cope in a world that might not see them as being special.

The steps incident

There are different views of steps from different ends of life

SOME time ago I was walking with my 25-year-old son through our local shopping centre. He and I were chatting as fathers and sons do when they're walking. We came to some stairs, perhaps twenty in total, that led up to a car park and I thought, I'm with my fit young son, and I do not want him to think of me as being old, so I'll walk up the middle of these stairs without so much as the aid of a handrail. He will be impressed with that. Or even if he isn't impressed, he won't think, Uh-oh, Dad's struggling.

So I did. A few metres before arriving at the first step, I made sure I was lined-up with the middle of the staircase even though I was secretly concerned as to whether my knees would hold out.

But far from being impressed with me walking up stairs beyond grabbing distance of a handrail, do you know what my son did? When we got to the bottom of the stairs, he placed his foot not on the first step but on the second step. Let me spell this out: he lifted his leg two steps from a standing position and then transferred his entire body weight—pivoted on a single knee joint and leveraged off quad and calf muscles in one leg—up two steps in a single, confident, sweeping action. His two-step lope was over and done within half a second. No big deal. It truly is a thing of beauty to watch a fit young man unconsciously display a feat of strength and orthopaedic agility that others can only dream of, and execute the same with the kind of grace and self-assuredness that only applies in the piquancy of youth. There was no hesitation. There was no furtive 'Where is the handrail?' look around. He saw stairs and thought, Why go one at a time when two at a time is so much more fun?

Now while being struck by this nonchalant display of physical fitness I was also of the view that perhaps there was a reason behind this two-step manoeuvre. Was there something on the first step that he didn't want to step in? Perhaps he wanted to get in front of me in order to turn and say something important? Was there a reason for performing this two-step levitation other than that, at twenty-five, you can? Apparently not, because he did the same thing again: another two steps in another single, effortless, muscular motion. Then another. And another. And all the while with hands in his pockets, head down and chatting away oblivious to how I was viewing the staircase. Before I knew it he was at the top and I was still plodding away in a fifty-something hold-my-breath-while-I-climb sort of way.

I have an observation regarding this incident. On the one hand there is tremendous parental pride in seeing a boy become a man with manly strength and capabilities. But on the other hand this was a confronting reminder of my own mortality. I too was once so fit that I didn't have to think about stairs. The twenties are a time when energy, vitality and sheer physical capability naturally spring forth. But by the fifties that physical frisson has long since passed, such that I am now reduced to secretly, pathetically, impotently thinking about how impressed someone might be that I don't have to use a handrail on a staircase. What lies ahead? Look at me: I can feed myself?

My son and I occupy different ends of the great crescent of life: he is on the windward side where the momentum of life pushes you forward towards career, relationships and the possibility of family. The fifties on the other hand straddle the slippery leeward side that leads inexorably to the sixties and whatever lies beyond. It's not about the stairs or indeed about my fit young son; it's about the passage of time and the shifting circumstances of life. The fact is that every stage of life has its trials: the young might struggle to find their pathway just as the old might struggle with stairs. Surely the important thing is to enjoy each stage of the life cycle and to savour and admire rather than to lament the passing of youth to the next generation.

6

Them and Us

DO you ever think that you are living in a parallel universe to others in your life? Do you ever ask yourself, Am I the only normal person on the planet? If so, then your daily musings can be characterised by a them and us world view. And it's nothing to be ashamed of. There are people in life who do not seem to get that you need to work in order to secure a particular lifestyle. Do you ever secretly marvel at how some people view the world? And then complain about being victimised because things aren't going their way. Do you ever silently compose great lectures to these people imagining that after a good 'telling off' they will not only mend their ways but acknowledge you as having been on the correct path all along? Are you still waiting for that moment and situation to arrive? There are some people— other people—who just do not get it. And there are those who do. We are the ones who do get it; they do not get it. Or is this world view better positioned in the chapter that talks about delusion?

Stumbles with a mumbler

Speak up or forever hold your peace

DON'T talk to me; I am still fuming. I have just come from a meeting with one of life's most frustrating creatures. That's right; I am talking about a mumbler. Don't look all innocent at me; you know exactly who I mean when I say a mumbler. There I am at a board table and mumble man is sitting opposite on a swivel chair. What does he do? Before he opens his mouth he swivels to the side, looks at the floor and then, in a barely audible, monotone voice, says something. Has he seen something on the floor? Is he speaking to me? Is he talking to himself? Has the meeting started? Is he speaking to someone via a Bluetooth device affixed to his ear?

At first I think it's me. I'm sorry, I didn't quite get that. Mumble man looks askance as if to say 'What's wrong with you?' but then he merely repeats the mumble. I can't ask him to repeat again. Can I? I lean across the table. I use my feet to inch the swivel chair to the side, moving like a crab so that I might pick up key words by reading his lips. But here's the thing. Mumble man has perfected the art of emitting a low-decibel mumble without actually moving his lips. A fusion of word-like sounds may tumble seamlessly from his mouth but I am still none the wiser as to what it is that he actually said.

This is a dangerous game, for there is only so long that you can fake it with a mumbler. At some point mumble man will expect a response; he will want proof that you have been listening. My mind works out what I would like to say: Look, mumble man, this isn't hard; sit up straight, look me in the eye and articulate your thoughts in audible and clearly understood sentences. Why do people avert their gaze when speaking? Is it a power game? The whole gaze-aversion thing puts me at a disadvantage because I am straining to hear. Why must I, as the spoken-to, struggle to understand what it is that the speaker is saying? I am in this meeting at your request, fella. Speak up.

But the existence of mumble man is only part of the problem I have with other people's volume control. Mumble man may well be too soft but at the other end of the spectrum there is a counter-balancing life form known as loud laughter guy. There I am at a restaurant, perusing the menu, when out of left field the air is cracked by a loud laugher. You know the sort. They are with friends at a restaurant and are more than mildly inebriated. Now I am a reasonable person, as you know. I like to be surrounded by people having a good time. But it annoys me when my good time is impinged upon by the good time of others and especially by intermittent outbursts of ear-piercing laughter. I don't mind if a table is boisterous as long as they are not abusive in language or behaviour to staff or diners. What I cannot stand is a group who lull you into a false sense of security by remaining quiet but who then proceed to burst forth with the shrill sound of ill-proportioned loud laughter. This is a restaurant; other people aren't carrying on like you; what makes you think you can despoil the quiet enjoyment of others by piercing the air with boorish, intermittent laughter? I'll tell you what it is. It's because some people have no external perspective on how they might be able to fit in with the behaviour of others. Time to mend you ways, mumble man and loud laughter guy.

Later on, life gets earlier

What's not to like about going to bed early?

THERE comes a time in life—okay later in life—when
you look forward to going to bed to, well, sleep of course.
Here's some advice for the young from the heady heights of
the land that lies beyond fifty. Not only is there a metabo-
lism shift that makes inbuilt fat burners go bung after forty-
five, but the body clock does a daylight savings shift after
fifty. Everything is moved back two hours so that 8 pm
feels like 10 pm, and 9 pm feels like 11 pm. That's why old
people—grandparents are notorious for this—have their
evening meal done and dusted before the six o'clock news.
Grandparents think it's time to go to bed after the *7.30
Report.* (Oh, I know it's called *7.30* but how can anyone grip
that title; it needs something like *Report* or *Project* to follow
to make it work within common language.)

I have a confession. I would like to be in bed by 9.30 pm
but even I think that's a tad old-mannish so I deliberately
stretch things out to what I think is a respectable hour. I
think you are officially across the line of middle age when
you operate on the premise that a respectable hour to go to
bed is 9.30 pm. But I can't help it, you see. And the reason
is that I am a complete and utter earlyist: I like to go to bed
early and I like to get up early. That's what we earlyists do:
we like to live life not so much on the edge but early and
very well prepared. No one catches us earlyists unawares.
No sirree. We're on time every time and we're proud of it.
Do you know what we earlyists like to do? We like to out-
early each other. 'So, you get up at 5 am, do you? Well,

that's a sleep-in for me. I'm already up by 5 am and I've done an hour's work. 5 am? Harrumph. Luxury.'

Sadly, not everyone sees the world through earlyist eyes. I am informed by generation Y that there are these places called nightclubs that do not kick off until 11 pm and that kick on until 3 am and later! Later than 3 am? On behalf of puzzled earlyists everywhere, let me ask: Does anything good happen in a nightclub after 3am? And if not, why do you want to be there? Actually, I have another confession. I do know of such places. I have witnessed them first hand. Not as a participant but as an observer. On the odd occasion when I have driven into my CBD office at 5 am, I have seen people streaming out of nightclubs. I am sorely tempted to one day turn up to one of this nation's hippest nightclubs at 7.30 pm, order my usual soda water (okay, with a dash of lime as I will surely be in a festive mood) and then sit back and soak up the atmosphere until, oh I don't know, say, 9.30 pm. At this time I suspect that I would stand, survey the scene, scoff pointedly and storm out thinking, Well that so-called night-club was complete dullsville. It doesn't measure up to what I expected. Imagine that. A fancy, funky nightclub dismissed by a fuddy-duddy earlyist for being tame. Yes, tame.

Now I know that you might think that earlyists like me are in fact a little bit boring, but let me assure you, earlyists are up for a bit of excitement just like late people. It's just that we earlyists like our excitement to be over by a respectable hour. And so it is for this reason that I think nightclubs need to broaden their market. How about instead of nightclubs we have early evening clubs designed for the hip and happening earlyist set? I want to change the image of the entire earlyist nation: we're actually not as prim and proper as you might expect; we like our action hot and sweaty like anyone else. (Okay, we prefer more hot than sweaty.) It's just that because of a body clock shift we prefer our action to fit between the end of the six o'clock news and 9.30 pm so that we can be fresh for work in the morning. Who's with me in my quest to reset the image of early people everywhere?

Cleanists, don't get too close!

I'm not a clean freak … however

I WAS at a petrol station the other day waiting in line to pay and as I got close to the counter I took special notice of the man in front. His hands were dirty. Not dirty as in an-honest-day's-sweaty-work sort of dirty (which I have no problem with) but dirty as in he-had-never-washed sort of dirty. And I thought, Gosh, am I glad I don't have to deal with this person in my life. And I say that because, well, I like clean people. I'm sorry if my Cleanist ways offend your politically correct sensibilities, but I do. Not only do I like people to be clean but I like people to smell clean. Not necessarily perfumed clean (which can be a deceitful sort of clean) but a real hot-soapy-water, underneath sort of clean (which is an honest sort of clean). If you understand what I have just said, then you too are a Cleanist.

Do you ever watch medical programs such as *ER* and feel jealous of the way surgeons get to use those lever taps to help them suds up with soap all the way to their elbows? To their elbows! No? Neither do I. Now, I don't want you thinking this Bernard Salt character clearly has problems: he is a clean freak. I am actually quite relaxed about a bit of dirt. Why, just the other day I left a dish in the sink overnight without rinsing it and putting it in the dishwasher. True story. Who knows what bacteria and insect vermin might have crawled all over the wicked, wayward, crumbly crumbs that sat on that dish, that paraded on that dish, that taunted me on that dish, all through the night. See? Not clean obsessed at all.

Anyway, these and other random thoughts were flitting through my mind as I inched towards the counter. And then it struck me. As dirty-hands guy was paying, he lifted his right index finger, which had been I know not where, and placed it on the keypad of an EFTPOS machine. It was as if I were in an Alfred Hitchcock movie. I had an out-of-body experience; I was on the ceiling looking down. I inspected the keypad. I felt sick. It was dirty. Not smudged dirty but dirty from the imprint of a thousand dirty-finger-guys dirty. And then it was my turn. I had to place my surgically clean finger on the same keypad as dirty-finger guy. I might as well have exchanged bodily fluids with this man right there and then. His germs were excitedly preparing to leap from the keypad on to my flesh. I had no cash. I had bought the petrol. I had to pay by EFTPOS. There was a line of people behind me. I was trapped in a petrol station dirt fest. I was on a conveyor belt to disease and infection.

As my finger pressed the keypad, I could feel a grittiness underneath which I am sure was the heaping of bacteria. I think you know me well enough by now to know that I am not a nutter sort of person. I am really quite normal. So my request is hardly unreasonable. Could petrol stations please place an anti-bacterial handwash by EFTPOS machines? That way I can rid myself of dirty-finger guys' bacterial residue immediately after my gritty EFTPOS experience. And no, of course I don't also require a wash basin with lever taps and hot, soapy water with suds that go right up to the elbow. Although if petrol stations wanted to install these of their own volition, then I wouldn't object. Fellow Cleanists, are you behind me in my campaign to limit the transfer of disease and infection through the wider use of anti-bacterial handwash? And if you are behind me on this, please don't get too close as I don't want any of your germs getting within leaping distance of my body.

Boring to Exciting? Dream on

Borings do the hard yards while others do lunch

I THINK there are two types of people in Australia that are simultaneously attracted to, and oddly repelled by, each other. Here's how it works. On the one hand there are people, like me, who live in the suburbs, go to work, pay their mortgage, pay their taxes, live in long-term, stable relationships and do their best to rear well-adjusted children. These people—let's call them the Borings—don't cause anyone any trouble. In fact I will go so far as to say that in terms of popular culture the Borings are invisible. No one is interested in the lives, the views, the relationships of the Borings. In fact go away; you are boring.

But what many do not understand is that the Borings are vital to the biological operation of another, far more glamorous life form that I like to call the Excitings. These are people to whom exciting things are forever happening. Drama and intrigue surround their every move and their every relationship. Even the Excitings' dreams are fascinating. In fact so fascinating that Exciting people like nothing better than to recount to Boring people what they dreamt about last night. And here we get to the essence of the symbiotic relationship that exists between the two humanoid life forms that inhabit the Australian continent. The *raison d'etre* for Boring people's existence is to serve as an audience for Exciting people. If the world comprised just Exciting people, then how would we know they were exciting? Exciting people need an audience and a benchmark.

Here's a confronting observation for Boring people. The only reason Exciting people hang around you is so that they can better define and admire their own exciting character. Your boringness confirms their excitingness. And the reason Boring people put up with this arrangement is because they like to feel needed. 'Oh woe is me, my girlfriend dumped me and (Boring person) I need consoling because I really did think she was the one.' Or, 'I thought I loved my boyfriend but he's just not in touch with his emotions and I don't know how to tell him. What should I do, Boring person?' And this is just the relationship side of the Excitings' lives. Exciting people are always having trouble on the work front. They are hounded by psycho bosses who just don't get them.

And perhaps because of their erratic work and relationship history, Exciting people are forever broke. But just when Boring people think, Poor Exciting person is having a hard time, the Exciting person is just as likely to announce that they are off to Europe on a three-month holiday. Excuse me, Exciting person, but I thought you were broke? This is a conundrum for Boring people, who thought they understood budgeting. If I want a three-month holiday in Europe and to maintain my house, car and all else that goes with that, here's how much money I will need. And here's how long I need to work to save that money. Exciting people, on the other hand, live in a world that operates independently of the financial principles that govern Boring people's behaviour. Money is an elastic concept in the Excitings' world. And when the Exciting person gets back from Europe, who do they pour out their heart to about being broke? Why, Boring people, of course.

I have often wondered whether it is possible to 'bat for the other side': for a Boring person to transmogrify into an Exciting person or vice versa? I have never seen this done and I suspect this is because at the heart of the Boring-Exciting schism is the sort of person you are. Although I must say that the Boring population seems to be in decline and that the Exciting population is on the rise. Perhaps this is a question that should be resolved at the upcoming census: would you describe yourself as Boring or Exciting? And if you are unsure, just apply this test: are you a teller of or a listener to dreams? Not only have I never told anyone what I dreamt about but the idea of recounting a dream to someone else is not something that would enter my head. Ergo I am a Boring person. I suspect my readership is also boring. Exciting people simply do not have the attention span to read a column such as this without someone telling them along the way what a fantastic job they are doing.

Don't resist the urge to do nothing

Doing nothing is doing something, isn't it?

DO you know what I did during the Easter break? Nothing. I know this is confronting to on-the-go sorts of people, but the fact is that I stayed at home for five consecutive days and I did nothing. I went nowhere. And I spoke to hardly anyone. I want the world to know that I had absolutely no noteworthy sporting, social or cultural experience over Easter and I refuse to feel guilty about it. Do you know what everyone at my work and in my street was doing while I was at home doing nothing over Easter? They were doing something. And when I say something I mean they were doing something really interesting and really exciting. They were away, up the coast or down the coast. Or they went interstate. Some went overseas. To Thailand, on Jetstar, for Easter. Can you imagine that? Now I know what you're thinking. You're thinking, This Bernard Salt is such a bore.

Bore? Me? *Au contraire.*

Let me tell you I did plenty in those five days. I cleaned the gutters. I mowed the lawns. I even cleaned the windows with proper window-cleaning stuff. And I went to Bunnings to get light globes. That was about as exciting as my Easter got. But progressively during those five days I had what can be described only as a spiritual awakening, a kind of revelation if you like. I realised towards the end of the break that with all of the jobs I was doing I was beginning to feel—how can I put this?—smug. Yes, *smug* is exactly the word for how I felt. Here I was doing all this work while others were whooping it up with Jetstar in Thailand. Perhaps I'm deluding myself, but I don't think I am. When all those dilettante holiday-makers got back from their holidays I know in my heart that they would have been mightily confronted by the pristine orderliness of my lawn and they would have immediately compared it with the shabbiness of their lawn. And they would have felt ashamed. Remember: every time a neighbour fails to keep up with another neighbour a garden gnome quietly dies somewhere.

But the Easter holiday-maker's anguish doesn't end with the great lawn comparison. No, no, no. Perhaps not immediately but eventually these people will also spot the cleanliness of my windows and mentally compare them with the smudginess of their windows. And while they can't possibly get up there to see, I have every confidence that by mid-May Easter holiday-makers will intuitively know that my gutters are unclogged and are just waiting for the next downpour to whisk water away efficiently. Be off my property, damned excess water, and never dareth ye to return. As you can see, such has been my revelation that I slip all too easily into biblical language.

But it's too late to repent, Easter holiday-makers. You can't possibly hope to achieve an elevated state of suburban enlightenment with the odd weekend clean-up. Who are you kidding? The next long weekend isn't until Queen's Birthday in June. Easter holiday-makers will just have to live with the decisions and the choices that they made to have a good time in April. I'm sorry, Easter holiday-makers, but that's the awful truth.

Sadly, I suspect that my way of thinking—there is value in doing nothing other than pottering around and maintaining the suburban home—is thinking from the twentieth century. The twenty-first century will be filled with more Easter holiday-maker types who see long weekends as experiential rather than as maintenance opportunities. And while that may well be so, that doesn't stop me taking inordinate pleasure in my clipped lawns, my clean windows and my unclogged gutters.

The agony and ecstasy of suburbia

The secret shame of a suburbia-phile

I AM a lover of suburbia and I refuse to be ashamed of how I feel. I have thought long and hard about this for quite some time. Should I disclose my feelings about the suburbs or should I continue to cover up? But how can I go on pretending that I don't have these thoughts, these feelings, these unbridled (yes, unbridled) passions? I am sure there are others out there who think the same way but are too afraid to speak out. And I can understand their reticence, for ours is a forbidden—some say unnatural—love, a love that can never be expressed let alone consummated in a politically correct world. Why, even admitting to quite liking the suburbs will undoubtedly draw the ire, the fire, and the castigation of Those Who Email. After all it is only deviants, heretics and other assorted ne'er-do-wells who are predisposed to—lip-curl and sneer—the 'burbs.

You do realise that outer suburbia is solely responsible for all global warming (as well as world poverty) and is full of isolated and lonely people who sit about all day just longing to live in an inner-city terrace house. That's right. But these poor outer-suburbanists (*Ausländers*, really) are forced—forced I tell you—to live deprived lives far from the civilising influences of the cafés, bars and restaurants frequented by—ssshh, here they come—The People Who Wear Black. You see it is the Black Clad Elite who understand how things really, really work. Or should work. The reason why people move to the outer suburbs is not because anyone wants to live there. Goodness me, no. The reason why people move to the suburbs is because they are forced to live there by big oil, by big banks, by big developers, by big polluters and by big tobacco. Yes, big tobacco, and don't ask why. They are all in cahoots. Oh, and one other thing about the Black Clad Elite. They are very sensitive to parody. Not parody of the suburbs; they love *Kath & Kim*. No, parody of the Black Clad Elite.

Are you beginning to understand why my love of suburbia is so fraught and forbidden? But this danger simply incites and frankly excites. I can think of nothing more fulfilling or frankly more thrilling than a Sunday drive through the suburbs. My car willingly embraces—no, hugs—the curves of winding residential streets replete with traffic pacifiers (what else could they be called but humps?), stopping here and dawdling there so I may gaze upon the Rubenesque splendour of a cul-de-sac's perfectly formed turning circle. To the suburbanist's mind there is nothing so pleasing as a Ramsay Street vista. The rollover kerbing is gently breached by a series of radiating driveways that all knowingly find their way to an amply proportioned double garage with workshop and storage area. Inside these dwellings I imagine a complete or blended family where people are employed and the kids are doing well at school and everyone is happy and life is comfy. Yes, comfy. It's suburban for comfortable.

I know this vision is confronting to The People Who Wear Black but I feel I owe it to my fellow suburbanists to explain exactly how we feel. Oh, all-knowing Black Clad Elite, can you not find room in your heart to permit the suburbanists to live out their lives free of lip-curl and sneer? No? They must be exterminated? Really? Run, suburbanists. Run for your lives. The Black Clad Elite are on to our wicked, wicked suburban ways.

Money Mortals miss the magic

There is little glamour to be had in staying within one's means

COME close boys and girls and get comfortable because I want to tell you story about the two types of people that inhabit this land. There are people like me, and I suspect you, although you can never be too sure about these things. We are known as the Money Mortals. To those of the Money Mortal tribe, money is a finite concept. There's a certain amount that comes in each week and there are bills that need to be paid and what's left over gets to be spent on anything we like. Now I don't want to go into troublesome concepts like taxation, but you get the basic idea. Money Mortals live in a world where a certain amount of money is all there is. There is no more. And there's no legitimate way to get any more.

So, do you know what Money Mortals do when they realise that only a certain amount of money comes into their household every week? That's right. They adjust their lifestyle to meet the available budget. *Budget*. That's a funny word, isn't it boys and girls? You don't hear many people talking of budgets these days. What you're more likely to hear about is how much money people deserve.

Now, of course, as I said at the beginning, there are two types of people. The counter-balancing force to the Money Mortals is a particularly glamorous and fast-growing tribe that goes by the name of the Money Magicians. Why, it wouldn't surprise me if there were lots of Money Magicians reading this right now. But the funny thing is that they don't know they're Money Magicians. Why are they known as Money Magicians? That's a very good question. It's because

Money Magicians can make money do all sorts of clever things that mere Money Mortals cannot. Money Magicians can make money stretch; they can make money materialise. Out of thin air. Oh, yes, they can.

For example, when a Money Mortal meets a Money Magician, the latter will say to the former how broke they are. And this makes Money Mortal feel sad for Money Magician. They've had a rough trot. Money Mortals also have rough times, but that's different; they don't need sympathy because, well, they're boring. And boring people do not attract sympathy. Sorry. But it's true. But then, a week after Money Magician was lamenting their financial destitution, do you know what happens? Guess. No, go on, I insist. Guess. Oh, all right. A week later, Money Mortal is apt to receive a postcard (or a Facebook status update) from Money Magician in, guess where? Guess. I bet you can't guess. Bali! That's right. Broke Money Magicians have secret powers that enable them to conjure up the funds to support the most outrageous lifestyles without having to do boring things like work and save and that nasty old b-word—budget. Boring people budget. Glamorous people go to Bali when they're broke. Don't you get it? Glamorous people deserve a bit of a break because they've had a bit of a rough trot. Not because they have worked and saved and budgeted, but because they're, you know, interesting.

Are you a Secret Money Magician? I suspect you are; why else would you be lolling about the house on a Saturday morning in your jarmies reading the paper rather than out there working? Try this test. When you get paid, do you allocate funds to the lifestyle you believe you are entitled to and then pay bills with what's left over? Or do you pay what needs to be paid and then make your lifestyle fit whatever is left over? It is really simple. In fact, this is such a simple concept that I think it should be the way everyone manages their spending, including governments.

Oh, I am having a joke with you, boys and girls: the idea of living within your budget is a matter for Money Mortals, not for glamorous types or for governments that are having a bit of a rough trot.

Pumcins are sweet on success

New tribes speak their own language

YOU'VE heard of Dinks (double income no kids), Yuppies (young urban professionals) and Kippers (kids in parents' pockets eroding retirement savings); now let me introduce you to the smashing Pumcins: professional urban middle-class in nice suburbs. You would be surprised how prevalent Pumcins are. Why, you could be part of the Pumcins set and you may not even know it. Try this test. Do you eat out at fashionable cafés? Yes. Would you describe yourself or your partner as a foodie? Yes. Have you been on a holiday to Noosa? Silly question. Of course. Do you secretly, or not so secretly, believe that you have some sort of affinity with the city of Paris? Yes. (Although having stayed there two nights on a 1980s Contiki tour is stretching the definition of 'affinity'.) Go to your refrigerator and see if on the top shelf or perhaps in a door shelf there is some—dead giveaway—goat's cheese. Yes? Well, hello Pumcins and welcome to the world of suburban aspirationalism.

If you have passed these tests then you will find the rest of my rules for admission to the Secret Society of Pumcins a cinch. Do you live in Sydney? Of course you do. Did you know that Sydney Pumcins have a secret code? Yes, they do. That code is hidden in the way aspirants pronounce a particular suburb's name. You do realise I could be shot for divulging this information. Keep this under your hat, but aspirational Sydneysiders pronounce the suburb of Mosman as Mozz-munn. If you listen carefully you can hear a bumblebee buzzing between the syllables of Mosman. At first I thought this was a Sydney peccadillo but then I heard similar in Melbourne. The bayside suburb of Brighton is pronounced by loyal Brightonians as Brah-ton. There is an aspirational ahh that links the syllables of Brighton.

This brings me to Salt's Law of Pumcins Pronunciation: the more fervently aspirational the Pumcins, the more pronounced is the Brighton ahh and the Mosman zzz. I suspect these vocal gymnastics are in fact part of a complex method of Pumcins communication. If a suburban aspirant talks about Mozz-munn or Brah-ton in a public setting, it is like a whistle set to a frequency that only other Pumcins can hear. Soon enough all Pumcins in the vicinity gather and chatter using their special language and eating their special food. Did I mention the goat's cheese? Don't underestimate the goat's cheese factor. I suspect there is something in the suburban aspirant's physiology that craves goat's cheese.

There are other rules, such as how you dress, which for men is straightforward enough: Polo, chinos and loafers. And please do not embarrass yourself by wearing a Bali knock-off Polo shirt. Female Pumcins can spot a fake Polo at 15 metres. Apparently it's in the stitching. The Italian loafers are interchangeable with boat shoes. No, you don't have to own a boat or even know how to sail. The idea is to

swan around New South Head Road or Toorak Road looking just a little bit nautical. Ahoy, Pumcins.

Do you have children? Really, three. Then get rid of one
because Pumcins only have two. And they are all doing
so terribly, terribly well for themselves in terribly, terribly
exotic locations in terribly, terribly important jobs. And,
really, they'd love to come back to Australia but there's
just nothing for them here. Brilliant. You are now speaking
fluent Pumcins. In one fell swoop you have communicated
to other suburban aspirants that you are so successful as a
parent that you have catapulted your kid into the global
economy. Welcome to the Australian Pumcins patch.

The cheesy barrier gets my goat

I feel trapped in the world of Pumcins and hipsters

HELP! Please help me. I can't get out. I'm over here. No, not
over there. Over here. Next to the café with tables on the
pavement. I'm trapped. I'm on the other side of the goat's
cheese curtain. What do you mean what's the goat's cheese
curtain? The goat's cheese curtain is a cultural divide that
separates the chichi inner suburbs (where there's goat's
cheese in every fridge) from the dreary middle and outer
suburbs in metropolitan Australia. My theory is households that eat goat's cheese do not eat McDonald's; they
are mutually repellent forces. Maccas will never release a
goat's-cheese-burger deal with Coke and fries.

The professional urban middle class in nice suburbs—
the Pumcins—are famously ensconced behind the goat's
cheese curtain. But also resident in this space are the

oh-so-green-thinking and the oh-so-black-wearing urban hipsters. What strange inner-city bedfellows the groovy hipsters and the corporate Pumcins make.

Gosh, I feel an *Oklahoma!* song coming on. Oh the Pumcins and the hipsters should be friends. One man likes to drive a Merc; the other likes to ride a bike. But that's no reason why they can't be friends. Pumcins dance with hipster daughters; hipsters dance with Pumcin gals. Inner-city folk should stick together; inner-city folk should all be pals.

And do you know why they should be friends? Because they share a distaste for that which lies beyond their realm. They have heard stories of strange beasts that live out there that go by the name of bogans and battlers, who live in habitats known as brick-veneers and McMansions.

The goat's cheese curtain may be a geographical divide but its influence is as much political, which means it's as green as it is cultural, and which translates into emulating a sophisticated Mediterranean lifestyle. Indeed, inside the goat's cheese curtain live alfresco foodie, artsy-fartsy types and a large helping of the business set. Apparently it is de rigueur to maintain a blog if you wish to be a hipster, and to own a pair of loafers (aka boat shoes) if you wish to be part of the Pumcins patch.

But what chaotic course does the goat's cheese curtain take through Australian cities? It's a bit like the Wallace Line that marks the meeting of the Australasian and the Asian tectonic plates through the Indonesian archipelago. There are distinctive flora and fauna on the islands of Lombok and Bali on either side of this fault line. The goat's cheese curtain similarly separates the Pumcins and the hipsters from the battlers and the bogans. I have studied the goat's cheese curtain in all the capital cities and find that the line is often marked by the presence of market umbrellas, by a plethora of pavement cafés and by more than a few minimalist homeware stores that smell of lavender and stock only white crockery and linen.

In Sydney the goat's cheese curtain extends north to Chatswood and south to Alexandria, with diversions to Bondi in the east and Leichhardt in the west. The heartland of this culture in Sydney, and quite possibly in Australia, is somewhere around Paddington. Melbourne's goat's cheese curtain covers similar territory: north to Brunswick, south to Elwood, west to Flemington and east to Richmond. Other cities don't have the critical mass to support extensive inner-city, chichi-lifestyle suburbs as such. Rather, in Adelaide this phenomenon is at best restricted to the island of North Adelaide, while in Perth it's the islands of Subiaco and Leederville. Yes, I do get Perth's Claremont thing, but Claremont is dominated by pure Pumcins. I have never seen a hipster in Claremont. Hipsters visibly wilt with distance from the CBD. Brisbane has a nascent goat's cheese curtain that stretches from South Bank through West End all the way to New Farm.

But all this doesn't solve my problem: how do I escape from inside the goat's cheese curtain? I own chinos. I have eaten smashed avocados drizzled with extra-virgin olive oil at a pavement café while wearing branded sunglasses. I have two pairs of boat shoes. Two! But fear not for me, because I have a cunning plan. Wearing a disguise, I intend to walk undetected through the goat's cheese curtain. My disguise? It involves a pair of Crocs, a terry-towelling hat, a pair of Stubbies and a polar fleece top that will carry me safely to the land that lies beyond the goat's cheese curtain.

7

Aspiration and Delusion

IF there is one thing that unites us all on the issue of daily mind-musings it our private aspirations and delusions. Of course it's possible for me to get that job, to own that house, to live that lifestyle, to 'be with' that person. Not that any of us actually spell out these private aspirations but they're there. And then there's the behaviour that belies the fact that an aspiration will never be achieved. I'm sorry but you will never own a two-storey, sandstone period dwelling in Sydney's Hunter's Hill no matter how much you admire the property pages. And even if you do dress in Lycra and buy clip-in bike shoes, you simply do not ride enough to be as fit as an Olympic athlete. Indeed looking the part is part of the delusion. Do you ever sit in a plane and at the slightest bump mentally project forward as to what might happen if the plane 'goes down?' When travelling overseas do you email and Facebook-post and blog to all and sundry because you're overseas playing the weary world traveller? Do you realise that no one actually cares what you think of the French people and countryside? But the fact that we go through these charades, these rituals, these behaviours suggests that we are all guilty of the kind of unspoken aspiration that preoccupies our thinking and which perhaps even leads to the occasional delusion.

The lure of whirring sprockets

You don't have to wear the uniform but it helps

THERE comes a time in every middle-aged male's life when
he can hear a voice calling him, beckoning him, luring him,
alluring him—all right, I will say it, seducing him—to ride
a bike. I have heard that voice and let me assure you it is
quite irresistible. I am a born-again cyclist, which means
that while I had a flirtation with cycling as a kid, I sort
of grew out of it—that is, until recently. And the reason I
have re-engaged with cycling is, I suspect, the same reason
every other post-fifty male takes up cycling: It's a way of
keeping fit if you have dicky knees. Or at least that's the
official line. The real reason men in particular are drawn to
cycling is because of all the cool bike gear you get to hang
out with: it appeals to the male sense of the mechanical. All
those sprockets and cogs whirring and clicking and spin-
ning in a direction controlled by the flick of a finger on the
handle bar of The Great Controller. Oh, yes, slight incline?
No worries, might just drop a gear and power on through.
It's all very exciting.

And this is to say nothing of the outfit that you get to
wear. In public! I am talking Lycra here. For those unfa-
miliar with Lycra, it's a stretchy fabric much favoured by
the sporty because it breathes and it hugs—grips really—
the human form underneath. In fact, this relatively new
phenomenon of middle-aged men taking up cycling has its
very own tribal acronym: this lot are known as MAMILs or
middle-aged men in Lycra. Now when I say I am a born-
again cyclist I am exaggerating a tad. I do have a bike and I

do get the whirring sprockets experience but I cannot quite bring myself to kit up in Lycra. I have looked at these outfits in bike shops but I just cannot bring myself to go all the way. I'm more of a shorts-and-T-shirt sort of cycling chap. I don't even have the mandatory pedal-clip-in shoes that make you walk funny when ordering a skinny latte at an outdoor café after a long bike ride. I wear runners. Runners! And my riding isn't on the open road in a fearless and fearsome peloton; it's a solitary experience on a suburban bike path, dodging walkers, kids, unleashed dogs and mothers pushing baby strollers. But I am not alone. There are other born-again cycling males just like me on the same bike path. We do not speak. We do not move in packs like the MAMILs. Our bikes aren't particularly fancy. And most damning of all, we don't wear Lycra. Shunned by the MAMILs, we are the forgotten and the apparently forgettable MAMISATs, or middle-aged men in shorts and T-shirts. We are cycling's outlanders who are destined to remain in bike-path purgatory until the day we overcome our fear of wearing Lycra.

But I suspect that day is not too far off for me. I find that I am already lingering amid the Lycra in my local bike shop. I have imagined myself in a brightly coloured outfit with a chic European sporting motif. *C'est si bon*. I have even imagined myself whizzing past walkers, kids, unleashed dogs and mothers pushing baby strollers on the bike path, who I am sure will look up and say to themselves: Hmmm, now there goes a very stylish MAMIL. Do I give in to the allure of the Lycra and go all the way with pedal-clip-in shoes? Or do I remain amid the humble but daggy MAMISATs who pedal for their own solitary purpose and pleasure?

A deluded boss's guide to functions

I know this is hard to believe but not everyone is enjoying the party

OCTOBER is when end-of-year drinks functions are planned. I can see it now. The boss leans back in his chair (most bosses are male), summons those who need to be summoned and suggests a drinks function for late November. The official reason for a drinks function is to thank staff, clients, consultants and other assorted hangers-on for their hard work throughout the year. That sounds plausible doesn't it? But that's not what's going through the boss's mind. What's going through his mind is a mini movie of the drinks function where he is the centre of attention. 'Oh Mr CEO what a wonderful event.' 'Oh Mr CEO how clever you are for running this business.' 'Oh Mr CEO do tell us another joke.' How do I know that this is what is running through the boss's head? Well, it's because I have made a study of these events for much of my corporate career. And I have made a note of the boss's behaviour at such functions.

Here's how it works. You get an invitation to a drinks function for 6–8 pm with speeches at 7 pm. The problem is that even if you arrive at 6.45 pm to ensure that you have to suffer through only fifteen minutes of excruciating small talk before speeches, the speeches do not actually start at 7 pm as promised. Do you realise how hard it is to steal a glance at your watch while chatting with someone? I have perfected the technique: I wait until their gaze has shifted and then sneak a split-second look at my watch before their gaze returns. Whenever I get away with this I feel I'm living life on the edge. The other way to check the time in a social situation is to glance at the wrist of the person you are speaking to. Sometimes you have to read a clock face upside down but this merely adds to the challenge.

It's 7.10 pm and still no sign of speeches. Where's the boss? You scan the room; there he is at the centre of a throng of fawners, sycophants and other assorted courtiers laughing uproariously at his every witticism. How can a balding, paunchy, middle-aged man with a bad case of dandruff and halitosis command such attention? In an instant I get what's happening. The invitation said speeches at 7 pm but the boss is having such a good time that he thinks everyone else is having a good time. No, we are not having a good time. You are having a good time because you are the boss. Can't you see that people who would normally dismiss you in a flash are fawning over your every word? Can't you see that? And do you know I suspect that many bosses can see precisely that. But they lap it up anyway.

But of course I am being unfair. Some bosses are not like that at all. A lot are, but not you. You're different. You're a special boss. Or at least I'm giving you an out to think that you're different. Some bosses at these functions are exceedingly diplomatic and are even on guard against those who would monopolise their time. Here's the modus operandi of a good boss at a drinks function: chat, chat, chat, move along, chat, chat, chat, move along. And they make sure they speak to everyone including the mailroom people. That's how it's done. And if you say speeches at 7 pm, then deliver speeches at 7 pm. I have a limited capacity for small talk, and after 30 minutes of drinking, middle-aged people need to find a loo. So I am told.

Eventually there is a speech. Please make it short. Please make it short. Look, it's not hard, Mr Deluded Boss. Thank everyone for their effort. Say a thing or two about the coming year. Make a piss-weak joke (in response to which everyone will laugh) and that's it. Easy. Do not ramble. Do not single out a favoured person. Do not start speeches late. Is it over? Can I go now? If I have made sure the right people have seen me, do you think I can work my way to the back of the room and depart? Done. I'm gone. I'm out of here.

Real-estatc desire does my head in

Is lust for real estate the newest deadly sin?

I WAS in Sydney this week, speaking at a venue in Hunters Hill. I'm not sure whether you know Hunters Hill but it's fair to say that it's kinda swanky. Posh, in fact. Now, as you know, I am a man of the world, or at least of Australia— okay, Melbourne. I may be a man of Melbourne but I have been to Hunters Hill before, so I knew what to expect. In fact, I have been to some of the swishest suburbs in every capital city in Australia, so I am not easily fazed. Melbourne's St Georges Road, Toorak, Sydney's Wolseley Road, Point Piper and Perth's Jutland Parade, Dalkeith, are the super-models of this nation's residential real estate. Gorgeous to look at but completely unattainable.

But as I was being driven through this particular street in Hunters Hill I looked out the window at the real estate and was struck by what I saw: grand period sandstone homes on wide, treed allotments and with filtered harbour and bridge views, all barely 6 kilometres from the CBD. It was all so close; the light so dappled, the eucalypts so fragrant, the housing so open; it was, fleetingly, perhaps attainable.

And do you know, in that heady moment my thoughts turned to a base, guttural, primal, carnal real-estate desire that has been with me all my adult life. I am ashamed to say that I have often coveted the real estate of others. Oh yes, yes, yes, I want to live in one of those houses; I want to possess every glorious inch of one of those houses.

In the days since that drive-by, Hunters Hill houses have been on my mind. In fact, I don't think I can move forward until I have had a serious relationship with one of those houses. Do you think, if I visited one of those houses, my obsession would ease? Or would a taste of this delectable real estate merely torment me further? I don't care. If you own one of those houses, please send photos. I have a secret. Yes, I live in Melbourne but I have had these feelings for Sydney's undeniably seductive real estate for years. It all started a decade ago with Elizabeth Bay. Oh, it was innocent enough. I went there for an interview and I was immediately smitten: gracious period homes with water views so close to the pulsing, nay, throbbing, heart of Sydney. And ever since then, whenever I'd pass anywhere near Elizabeth Bay I'd look wistfully at the near perfect real estate and sigh a Melbourne sort of sigh. But after last week's experience, I have to say that I have finally moved on. It's nothing Elizabeth Bay has done or didn't do. It's me. I've changed. My real-estate feelings have shifted to another. And that other is Hunters Hill.

From the seclusion of my car I wondered what sort of people owned houses like that. I fantasised about knocking on the door and asking each resident how it was that they came to own such real estate. I even reasoned that they would give one of two possible responses. They might say that they had inherited the lot. Or it might be that they are simply smarter, work harder and have been prepared to take more risks in life than I have. I prefer the first imaginary response. It absolves me from the responsibility of being unable to sate my clearly carnal real-estate desire. The second response is problematic. Using the real estate you own by middle age as a metaphor for success in life is a dangerous and confronting proposition. Far better to simply say that we all have different opportunities in life and make different choices.

So, when you are next in the vicinity of particularly alluring, intoxicating, seductive real estate, could I suggest that you merely acknowledge the beauty and keep on driving by. Otherwise, let me assure you, it completely does your head in.

The rise of super shock syndrome

Retirement planning can become an obsession

I AM told by those close to me that I am a man obsessed with the riveting subject of superannuation. Not your superannuation. Good heavens no. I am obsessed with my superannuation. And the reason is that I have so much superannuation it's a little bit embarrassing. In fact I'm thinking of ways I can give some of my hard-earned and hard-saved superannuation to the government so that they might do something really, really useful with it. I mean if I get to keep the lot I'll probably just fritter it away on a retirement lifestyle.

You do realise I am being facetious when I say that. No one says, 'I have too much superannuation.' No one. For many years I had no real idea of my superannuation balance. I just assumed that, well, I was working hard and was being paid reasonably well and that smart accountant types had worked out if I put away the 'standard super plus a bit' it would all sort itself out in the end. So I thought I could live on my super forever because, well, I had been paying into super forever. And besides, really, what young person can be bothered with the subject of superannuation? A super discussion is an absolute snore-fest for anyone under the age of fifty.

Then something quite remarkable happens on your fiftieth birthday. Yes, yes, your knees go. Yes, yes, your hair thins. Yes, yes, your waist thickens. But in addition to these visible signs of ageing, there's another bizarre physiological transformation that takes place. Suddenly discussion about renovations no longer excites. No matter how minimalist the design and how white-with-black-trim the colour scheme. And nor does discussion about the behaviour of other people's children and the parlous state of other people's relationships. Rather, the discussion that is most likely to excite the passions beyond fifty is a full-on and frankly unfettered financial chat about the tax advantages of superannuation. And rightly so. Do you realise how tax effective superannuation is?

I have a theory that at some point in the near future millions of working baby boomers will come down with what will be known as super shock syndrome. This is a recognised medical condition that impacts precisely three years in advance of retirement. This is when pre-retirees work out the annual cost of their lifestyle and the annual income that can be supported by their superannuation. The raw, naked, visceral difference between these two figures becomes apparent in a single moment of financial clarity. This is when super shock syndrome first strikes. The symptoms begin with profuse sweating, then anxiety sets in and this is followed by fear then anger. 'But … but … I've worked hard, saved, contributed to super. You mean to tell me that all that effort delivers this paltry sum to live on?' I predict that by the middle of this decade super shock syndrome will be the most fashionable affliction for the over-fifty set.

Of course there is no cure for super shock syndrome. And with more and more people pouring into this time in the life cycle, there is a national problem ahead. But then I have no doubt that those kindly generation Xers and those good-sport generation Ys will come to the fore and happily help out by paying more tax. Okay, okay, so they might officially grumble a bit about this but deep down we boomers know that they wouldn't have it any other way. This lot will pay more tax so that the horrible effects of super shock syndrome might be alleviated through the more generous pensions, benefits and concessions that will be doled out by politicians seeking boomer votes. Isn't democracy a wonderful thing?

And yet the funny thing is this. No matter how much superannuation you have, and no matter how generous is the concession and benefits support network, I suspect that all this still won't be enough to meet the retirement lifestyle expectations of the baby boom generation.

Travel broadens the mind

Colonials love nothing better than emailing or simply checking in from overseas

HOLA amigos. Do you know where I am at this very moment? Guess. I bet you can't guess. I'm in España. On holiday. That's right I'm living it up in the Spanish sea-side village of San Sebastian while you lot are freezing in another Australian winter. Would you like me to send you a postcard? I'll send you a postcard. And I have a travel blog, too. Do you want the address? I'll email you my blog address. Would you like me to buy you a present? I'll buy you some Spanish cava. Did you know that cava is like champagne, but they can't call it champagne because of the French, so they call it cava? See how sophisticated I have become; that's what happens when you travel—you learn so much. What is the point of an Australian going on an overseas holiday if there is no opportunity to go on and on about it to other people? That's why we still send postcards back to the office. (That reminds me.) But then has it not always been so for colonial Australians who are constantly aware of their isolation from the centre of the world?

The English talk about going abroad, which means to the continent. And it's fair enough. Jumping on a Dover ferry to buy cheap booze in Calais hardly qualifies as going overseas even though that is technically what they are doing. To the English *overseas* means the US or Australia. And I think the same logic now applies to Australians. In the old days going overseas meant taking a slow boat to Southampton. Today, with the increasing accessibility of international air travel, a number of intervening destinations have opened up. And frankly the entire process is messing with Australians' heads.

I propose there is such a thing as a going-overseas line that is expanding outwards from the Australian continent. The idea of going overseas used to start when the boat left the heads at Sydney Harbour or Port Phillip Bay. I don't think going to New Zealand qualifies any longer as going overseas. And the same goes for Bali, Fiji and any island in between. In fact, I think the going-overseas line now extends to Singapore. And I might add that there are other places on a downgrade watch from being considered overseas destinations, such as Hanoi and Bangkok. We need a new term to describe nearby destinations. Something like *abroad* would be good: we must first travel abroad in order to travel overseas.

Regardless of where overseas starts and finishes, there is a ritual that must be performed by every Australian upon their return. As soon as they clear customs and exit into the arrivals hall to waiting relatives, it is mandatory that said travellers duly and solemnly declare something along the lines of: 'I have travelled the globe and have come to the conclusion that Australia is the best place on earth.' These words must be said even if you've just spent a long weekend at Kuta Beach. And at this point the assembled relatives nod in unison before asking important stuff like what movies were watched on the plane.

But enough about you and your trip. Now back to me. Do you want to see my photos? Here's a picture of our hotel, and that room on the top right is our room. I've circled it. It was so close to the pool. If you ever go you should definitely try to stay in that room. And if you ever need a driver I've got the perfect person. He took us to his home and we got to see how the locals really live. Did you get my postcard?

No appetite for fanciful posh nosh

The food industry takes itself way too seriously

YOU do realise the moment I say what I am about to say I will be vilified from pillar to post across the blogosphere.

And the reason I am to be flailed—or should that be fricasseed?—is because I want to register my complete and utter boredom with cooking shows, celebrity chefs and their fawning, hawing, baying acolytes, the trendiest and the newest inner-city life form: the foodies. Why are some people inordinately proud of their foodie status? I like maps. I don't feel the need to inform people that I'm a bit of a mappie. But not foodies. They feel the need to advise all and sundry of their affliction not just with food but with fine food. I'm a foodie and I eat only exotic food. I'm a foodie and I eat dukkah. I'm a foodie and I know what dukkah is and you don't, so there. I'm a foodie and I can't digest anything that hasn't been plated up correctly. I'm a foodie and I use phrases such as 'plated up correctly'. Do you know there are some depraved people in this world who eat their meals off—hushed tone—coloured plates.

'No, they don't.'

'Yes, they do.'

'But, but ... how can they possibly appreciate the delicacy of the diced red chilli set against the soft, pink flesh of the prawns (drizzled with tangy lime juice) and the iridescent green of the coriander unless it's plated up on a white plate? And preferably a white plate that's rectangular to show everyone that they are just a little bit arty?' Well, my fine foodie friends, that's probably because they don't eat chilli lime prawns or maybe it's because they don't particularly care what their meal looks like. Maybe to some people it's just a meal. Maybe to some people they've got more pressing things in life to deal with than to pontificate about the artistry of plating up.

I am often at fancy restaurants for work throughout the week, and when I get home on a weekend, do you know what I want to eat? Tomatoes on toast. On my knees sitting in front of the television. Bliss. And, no, I don't want melted goat's cheese or drizzled olive oil on the tomatoes. I just want plain food that doesn't cost an arm and a leg and that is quick to prepare. It is not a crime, foodie people, to occasionally want food that is plain, quick and cheap. No, really, it's not. I've checked with the police.

And do you know what else I can't stand about foodie culture? The posh restaurants. I'm sick of them. And I'm especially sick of their waiters. 'Hi, my name's Tom and I'll be your waiter tonight.' And Tom then goes through interminable theatrics where he lovably tries to remember what's on the specials list. Hey, Tom. I've got an idea. Why don't you type out the specials on a piece of paper and attach that list to the menu? What, and deprive Tom, who thinks he's an about-to-be-discovered actor, of his moment of glory when he says '… and we've got some Coffin Bay oysters'? Coffin Bay oysters? Really? That's good because me being such a foodie and all I wouldn't touch those trash oysters from Streaky Bay.

The game's up, foodies. It's time not so much for a slow movement in food but for a plain movement in food. Nothing schmancy. Just plain food that doesn't have to be plated up correctly and doesn't involve a drizzling.

How to handle a ConDom

Some people are oblivious to their conversational dominance

I have had it up to here; I cannot take it anymore. Has no one on this planet ever heard of the concept of conversational balance? The apparently novel idea that a conversation is a two-way experience; that one person should not dominate the oxygen, the airwaves, the aural space within a social-chitchat-circle situation. If you are at a drinks function and there are four people in a circle and you are chatting and you have chatted for more than sixty seconds uninterrupted, then read this and understand that you are an interminable bore. You heard me. A bore. No, the fact that you think your stories are interesting is not an excuse. No, the fact that no one else speaks up if there is a silence is not an excuse. The reason why everyone in the social chitchat circle falls silent on the rare occasion that verbiage is not spilling from your mouth is because we are all shell-shocked. We think that if we were to say anything that you would interject with 'That happened to me yesterday but only worse ...' and then you would commandeer the conversation in your direction. Yet again.

Where do Conversational Dominators, or ConDoms for short, get off? No, ConDoms, your lives, your children, your partners, your holidays, your family dramas, your illnesses, your outfits and where you got them are not exciting. They are in fact mundane. The reason why we of the social chitchat circle appear interested in what you have to say is because we are dazed by your self-absorption. We are thinking, This ConDom's eyes are really close together. We are thinking, This ConDom has a bit of spit on her upper lip that is about to project towards my open drink. Better shift my drink to the other hand. We are thinking, This ConDom's got a bulging vein just to the left of her left eyebrow. Do you know what we of the social chitchat circle are not thinking? We are not thinking, This is a fun person to have in our midst. We are not thinking, Gosh my life is boring in comparison. We are not thinking, Please tell us about your Noosa holiday. Oh wait, you have photos on your iPhone? And you're going to get them out and you want us to say something about each of your photos? All one hundred of them? This is brilliant. Hardly anyone has been to Noosa so photos offer such an insight. And besides, it's educational to see how other people live, don't you think? I see. I see. Hmmm. Hmmm. And here you are in Hastings Street shopping because it was the one cold day in tcn that you had and, yes, everyone does need a break from the beach and, yes, you did tell me that you bought a new outfit but that when you got back to Melbourne it just looked so wrong. Well, well, well, that is all just so interesting. Thank you, thank you, thank you Ms ConDom.

The problem with Conversational Dominators is that they are not always apparent. Sometimes they sneak up and before you know it they are in the thick of things commanding attention. They start off all slow, asking you about your life, but then at some point, maybe five minutes into proceedings—perhaps when they adjudge that the audience has reached peak readiness—they spring into life. It might be alcohol related; there's a tipping point in an evening when the shackles come off and the Conversational Dominators break out.

This leads me to my point: how to survive a social chit-chat circle by early recognition of a ConDom. Actually there are two types: there's the pure Dominator type, who will simply not shut up, and then there's the Commandeering type, who will allow others to speak but only for fifteen seconds before they interject. And they really need to do this because whoever was speaking was really not that interesting. If you should spot a Conversational Dominator in your midst, then do as I do. Be sociable up front but then politely, discretely, purposefully excuse yourself the minute they start doing their stuff. Nothing deflates a ConDom quicker than a diminishing audience.

The scent of a man can be a close shave

Why can't a man comment on another man's aftershave?

Okay, I want you to take a deep breath and sit down, for I have a tale to tell that will shake you to the core. As it did me. I am still traumatised by the experience. Yes, traumatised, I tell you. I still carry the scars.

Earlier in the year I was at an event where I had to have my photograph taken. The photographer suggested we go in his car to a street three minutes away to get a better context for the picture. Which we did in no time at all. As we were driving back in his car he said, 'I like your aftershave.' Let me repeat that. Two men, alone in a car chatting about nothin', looking straight ahead, and one man says to the other, 'I like your aftershave.' Do you know, in my fifty-plus years of life, no male has ever said that to me. I have had the odd woman say it—usually after an air kiss, where she gets her nose close to where aftershave is sprayed—but no male. When you deconstruct this statement—'I like your aftershave'—there is nothing inherently offensive about it. It did not contain any offensive language. And it was not an improper suggestion. But I am sure that all males reading this, no matter their orientation, would find such a comment confronting.

Ah, but my fine photographic friend did not leave it at that. And, no, I didn't encourage him or lead him on. In reply, I resorted to the *Handbook of Bloke Comments for Every Occasion* and mumbled something like 'Oh' or 'Argh' or 'Err' or the ever-popular 'Err-argh'. I do recall keeping my head orientated towards the windscreen. Do not flinch. Do not glance sideways. Do not move. Such a powerful phrase, don't you think? 'I like your aftershave.' After my eloquent response, he went on to say something else. I could see and feel it coming. He was going to say something else. Oh my god, what is he going to say? Please, no red lights. Please, make the car go faster. Why is this car going so slowly? Please, God, let me teleport myself out of this situation and back to the safety of the herd. And then he said, without any sense of tension or embarrassment, 'It's Chanel, isn't it?'

Oh my god, he's asked me a question. Oh my god, not only did he compliment me on my aftershave but he guessed it right. What sort of man comments on another man's aftershave? What sort of man can tell from a car-seat distance that the scent on another man is none other than Bleu de Chanel? I'll tell you what sort of man: a bloke who knows his fragrances, that's who. So what if this guy recognised my aftershave? Maybe I wear too much? But it's 11 am. I put it on over four hours ago. And I only use a bit. No, he's wrong. Not me. I should have complete sovereignty over my aftershave. I shouldn't have to defend my right to complete fragrance anonymity. Bleu de Chanel was my private little secret. Now, thanks to photographer scent guy, it's out there for all the world to see and smell.

Then again, it is possible that I might be just a tad paranoid about this. This bloke was perhaps twenty-five. Maybe that's what generation Y men do: they swap thoughts about fragrances. I cannot recall what I replied when he identified my aftershave, but I suspect it was something along the lines of my response to his initial comment. I must have blacked out from fright—or from tension. In either case, eventually we arrived back to the group and nothing more was said about what was said in his car just a few minutes earlier.

Flights of fancy landing

How to safely land a plane from the passenger seat

I FLY a lot between Melbourne and Sydney for work, and have done so for twenty years. And I must say that I have noticed something quite odd about aeroplane behaviour during the past seven or eight years. In the old days planes took off and landed smoothly. Planes used to be a lot like buses: you'd get on, and unless you were sitting in a window seat, you wouldn't know you were not on a bus. Not like today. Planes take off like a slingshot; they seem to want to get as high as possible as quickly as possible. I suspect it has something to do with noise abatement.

But this isn't the worst of it. On flights from Melbourne to Sydney it's almost as if the pilot gets to the destination airport before realising we are pointing in entirely the wrong direction. This requires a series of sharp left-hand turns to straighten up. Not only that but the pilot also seems to realise at the last minute that we are indeed way too high so we need to dive as well as turn. Psst, Mr Pilot, why don't you ring ahead when you get to Goulburn and straighten up 200 kilometres out? Sheesh, I don't know; do I have to think of every solution?

Anyway, even though I am an experienced flyer, I will confess to occasionally getting a tad nervous, especially on approach to Sydney with all that twisting and turning and diving. I get these irrational mental images of the pilot suffering a massive heart attack mid-turn and dive, and of the copilot trying to move him from the joystick, which is jammed in the downward position. Whatever will we do? We're all gonna die! Fear not, for I have the situation in hand. Immediately and telepathically grasping the seriousness of the situation, I put my dive-fixing technical response into operation. If the plane is spiralling out of control to, say, the starboard side—that's the right-hand side for you landlubbers—I press my right foot hard into the plane's floor and make a braking action. At the same time I shift my entire weight from my right buttock to my left buttock so as to counter-balance the plane's tipping. I also grit my teeth while doing both.

Don't say it; let me guess. You're thinking: How can a single passenger making a braking motion with his foot and shifting his entire weight to one side of the seat possibly pull a plane out of a hopeless death dive? Well, normally I would agree with you but not on this occasion. Being the highfalutin statistical sort of person that I am, I can only point to the undeniable fact that on every occasion I have done this, the plane has righted itself. The proof is in the pudding or, as we superhero passengers like to say, in the fact no plane that has been subjected to my floor-pressing and weight-shifting has gone down.

At the end of the flight, when all the passengers dutifully file past the flight attendants and say goodbye, I usually like to give them an 'Aw shucks, it was nothin' look. And, do you know, I know they know it was me and my floor-pressing and weight-shifting that saved the plane because, as I leave, they give me a funny 'Who was that man?' look. And as I walk up the aerobridge I give my heels a little double click, thinking I just know I'm going to have a great day in Sydney.

A day to say thanks for nothin'

Oh for a day to do nothing in particular

I CAN keep my secret not a moment longer. I have manipu-lated the system. I have misled others as to my whereabouts for no good purpose other than to sate my carnal desire for, well, this is hard for me to talk about. You see, I have these thoughts that will not go away. Oh all right, I will tell you. I think a lot about time off, time out, time to myself, time to do as I wish, time that is my own. I yearn for time. Me time. Not you time. Me time. All right? Happy? Now leave me alone.

The secret time that I want to talk about was last week. I was in London. For work. Arrived on the Tuesday. Meetings and workshops for three days. Finished up in the city on the Thursday afternoon. Should have taken a cab to Heathrow and caught the 10.30 pm QF10 to Melbourne. But I didn't. I deliberately and with malice aforethought stayed on. In London. For twenty-four hours longer than was absolutely necessary. By myself. No one to answer to. No one at me. No one asking me to do stuff, to say stuff, to send stuff, to be stuff. You can see the scale of the guilt I have been carrying all week. I really can identify with the tortured souls of mass murderers: guilt is a horrible thing.

And do you know what I did with this so-called day off in London? Okay, if you insist, I will tell you. Are you sitting down? I don't want you to be shocked. Here it comes. What I did in London on my day off is nothin' in particular. Get it? I totally wasted my free day in London. Oh I still can't quite believe it. A rush of adrenalin courses through my veins whenever I think about it. To have so much time that you can actually wantonly, shamelessly, recklessly waste it is luxury. Oh yes, yes, yes, give me time every time; it doesn't have to be a good time, and yet with a surfeit of time I am satisfied, I am sated, I am suddenly relaxed.

Now before you get all judgemental let me assure you there were others involved in this subterfuge: my PA (can't get nothin' past her even if I try) and my family (ditto). You do realise that my family and my PA are in cahoots. Oh yes. They don't know that I know but I do know. They are in cahoots to get me to take time off. For my health. For my state of mind. Work-obsessed, so they say. Becoming paranoid, so they say. Me? Work-obsessed? Paranoid? Rubbish. Why, I will have you know that I breezily and just a little too easily took a sick day in September 1992. Okay, so I was feverish and sweating and spent the day in bed, but that's not the point. The point is I rang in sick. And what's more I am planning to take another sick day at some stage during the 2010s. Tsk tsk, I do so enjoy livin' life on the edge.

Now when I say I did nothing in London, that is not entirely true. I went for a walk. Up Regent Street. I sat in Green Park, ate a sandwich, had a cup of tea and I watched people. For quite a long time. I may be on the wrong track here, but judging by the ease with which others were doing what I was doing, I suspect there are people who do this sort of thing quite often: they sit and they watch people for, oh, perhaps minutes on end. I even bought a tie from a men's shop on my walk. I never buy ties. I buy suits and ties together, but never just ties; it's a more efficient way of buying. Yes, we men think in terms of the efficiency of the tie-buying process. But that protocol went out the door on my day off in London.

Do you think I could do this again? You know, take a day off? Perhaps in Melbourne? Too damn right I can, and I will. Now I don't want you to spread this information but I am planning to take another day off in March 2015. Ho ho ho, I do so like this new, more relaxed Bernard. He's my kinda guy: so loose, so easygoing; not work-obsessed at all.

8

Men and Women

NOWHERE is the concept of matters that matter better evidenced than in the subject of men and women and intimate relationships. This is where the daily musings work overtime, where people of both genders scope the possibilities and the problems associated with being together. Some have worked this out in a very modern way by living apart together; known as LATs, these couples swear they are better apart than together. Others couples live together without the immediate prospect of marriage. Known as cohabiting lovers uncommitted to marriage or partnership (or Clumps), these couples offer a brand new take on the model of male–female relationship. But everyday thought isn't always about the intimacy of relationship; it is more often than not about the practicalities. Do you know why women give men new clothes for Christmas? It's so that men will look smart for the photos. And do you know why men look after the barbecue? It's because women like to give them a job that is self-contained and removed from the real action that takes place in the kitchen.

The delight of couples living apart

Some couples do it from different locations

ONE of the most common household types in Australia is mum, dad and the kids, otherwise known as the traditional nuclear family. Here is a life form that has come to typify Australian suburbia. In less enlightened times such families were based around dad being the wage-earner and mum looking after the children. Today this model has altered: both mum and dad do paid work and both, notionally at least, share the responsibility of child rearing. There are variations on this model, including one-parent families and gay-couple families. In some families it's mum who works and it's dad who looks after the kids. And while all this morphing of the family into a variety of options is all very interesting, I think the most important variant is the LAT or living apart together model.

Forget gay marriage. That's old hat. The newest social trend is for couples to live together apart, which necessitates separate households. Fly-in fly-out mining has been a recent manifestation of the trend, but what I am talking about is extreme LAT behaviour. I was struck some years ago by a conversation I had with a professional woman in her late thirties who was in a happily committed relationship but who lived separately from her partner. Now, of course, we all understand that there are times in a couple's relationship where work takes one person away for a period of time. Indeed living separately might also occur for a time after hooking up (as generation Y says) because it takes a few weeks, okay months, to dismantle at least one household and to fuse a single, happily conjugal place of residence.

But the arrangement this woman spoke of was very different. She had met her partner later in life—she in her late thirties, he in his mid-forties. They both had had unsuccessful committed relationships previously. They were both career people. They both worked in the CBD. They both had established apartments and had come to enjoy their busy modern lives and lifestyles. You can see where I am going with this. The upshot is that they are together as a couple. It's just that they both like their independence and therefore retain separate households. I might add that there were no children involved in or planned for this relationship. Now I do get this. Why would a successful career woman give up her lifestyle to merge her lot with someone else? She had worked out that the best arrangement was for both to retain separate lives and apartments but within walking distance of each other.

Now, I know what you're thinking, as indeed this is exactly what I was thinking as she was outlining her arrangement. Apparently they have sleepovers at each other's apartments and—this is the thing that surprised me—there is no schedule. Clearly this arrangement is not for someone like me. I like certainty. I'd need to know that on Wednesday it's your place and on Thursday it's my place. I'd have a roster on the fridge door at both apartments! That way both partners know where they stand. But the whole arrangement goes beyond sleepovers. Do they do a bit of a whip-around to clean up before their committed partner arrives? Isn't that contrary to the charter of a committed relationship?

With more career couples re-partnering later in life, I can see a market for this: if you are a 45-year-old with some relationship history, you might be a tad cautious about tossing in your lot with an unproven but I am sure delightful lover. It's a way of hedging your bets. But of course you can't say to your committed lover, 'Look, darling, I want to hedge against the possibility that you and I might not work out so I've decided to keep my household separate.' No, of course it's not that I am not committed; in fact, what I am proposing is the latest fashionable kind of relationship: we will be living apart together. Somehow I think we'll be seeing a whole lot more LAT relationships in the post-45 and especially the post-55 market over the coming decade.

Presents of mind are a gift for women

Never mess with women's gift-giving protocols

PSST, fellas. Over here. Keep your voice down and act natural. I don't want them to see us consorting. What do you mean, 'Who's them?' Why, women of course. They see us blokes talking and they will want to know what we're talking about. If we do get sprung, our story is this: we were talking about our feelings for the womenfolk in our lives. He he, they will love that.

Now down to business. Fellas, I have a revelation. Are you sitting down? My revelation is that women are involved in the regular exchange of gifts. Yes, gifts. They give each other gifts for all sorts of reasons and we men have had no idea of what's been going on. That is until now. For years I have been going about my business quietly noting the female practice of gift giving. I was nearly spotted once but I pretended to be a dumb male, and can you believe I got away with it? Me? A dumb male? Precisely. Now I know what you're thinking, fellas. You're thinking: Gift giving? What's so revelatory about gift giving? Presents for the kids on their birthdays and again at Christmas. What's hard about that?

Oh dear, the naivety of some men would be kind of sweet if it weren't so sad, right, ladies? Women know exactly what I'm talking about. Men are in the dark on the matter of gift giving and that's exactly the way women like it. And the reason is that if men knew the extent of their partner's gift-giving ways, there would be a revolt. Or at least a hissy fit of some description. You know how it goes. He sulks all day ranting about the cost but by dinner he has calmed down.

Gift giving—the great social currency of our time—is conducted entirely by women and entirely for women. Oh, you think that present delivered to a kid's birthday party is for the kid? No, it's not. That kid's birthday present is one woman talking to another woman. The care, the creativity, the cost, the wrapping are all part of a complex social and diplomatic exchange that takes place between women. A good present says: 'I approve of my kid socialising with your kid.' A perfunctory present says: 'I am yet to be engaged by you or your child.' Look, fellas, you can scoff all you like, but I am right on the money with this one. Women give gifts to their kid's friends, to their friend's children, to their nieces and nephews, to their kid's teacher at the end of the year (yes, fellas, it's true) to say nothing of coaches, music teachers, hairdressers (yes, hairdressers, for there is a special bond between women and those entrusted to cut their hair) and other assorted hangers-on.

In fact, so prevalent is gift giving among women that they keep spare gifts in special places in the house just in case. Some have emergency gifts for when they are gift ambushed. Yes, gift ambushed; women talk like this. Do you know, fellas, who women give their most considered gifts to? Ha ha ha, fellas, you can be so funny. No, it's not you. It's their best friend, their BF, their bestie, the person they speak to every day to canvass the errant and sometimes egregious behaviour of their children, their extended family and invariably their husbands. These bestie's gifts are special gifts. I have sighted these gifts. They involve soap and smell of lavender and are bought at special shops frequented by women.

And, what's more, these special gifts require what is known as special wrapping. White paper is popular, as is gold or black. The paper must crease neatly; no crinkles. Crinkly paper is an affront to the recipient's sensibilities. Sometimes the gift is wrapped again in clear cellophane. Don't ask me why but this is crucial to the special wrapping process. Then comes ribbon or black string or something that looks like grass but which goes by the name of raffia and then a sprig of, say, rosemary or a stick of cinnamon. Again, I do not know the significance of all this, but what I can say is that it is vital. How do I know this? I know this because I once offered to wrap just such a present and was summarily dismissed because men don't do it right. And, do you know, this suits us blokes just fine. Life is simpler and happier when men are kept oblivious to the gift-giving currency that underpins modern Australian households.

Men defy the scourge of chitchat

Men have a predictable range of small-talk options

I HAVE a theory about telephones and men and women. Women love phones; men hate phones. The reasoning behind my theory is this: women are social creatures who see communication as an end in itself. Men are different. Men are hunters who prefer warrior hand signals to actual speech: 'Me see mammoth; me go in for kill; you move downwind; in fact good idea you stay downwind long time.' I reckon most men could quite happily communicate the preceding phrase about killing a mammoth without uttering a word. I've got it all worked out: two fingers pointing to eyes means 'me see'; pinch nose means 'you stay down wind'.

For women social communication can ramble in any direction and—get this, fellas—it doesn't have to reach a conclusion. Men do not understand this. Why discuss something without seeking an outcome? Why stalk a mammoth without killing it? I don't want to know how the mammoth is feeling or what it is thinking. I have it on good authority that women ring their female friends more or less weekly for a chat. And that some women speak to their mothers and/or sisters daily. In fact many times daily. Do you know, I have never received a phone call from a male friend for a chat-without-a-purpose? Ever. Or if I have, I have deleted the experience from my memory bank. In fact, I have trouble even conceptualising how such a conversation would go.

'Hey, Bernard, how are you?'

'Fine thanks, Bazza, and you?'

'Good. Good. See those Sainters won again on the weekend.'

'Yep, they're on a roll.'

'So, Bernard, how's life?'

And it is at this point that I am thinking: What is the purpose of this call? Why is Bazza acting weird? What does he mean 'How's life?' What exactly is he implying? Is

Bazza implying that I don't have a life? I'm going to have to kill Bazza.

In fact, man-to-man telephone conversation needs to establish right up front who is calling, the purpose of the call and how long the call is likely to take.

'Hi, Bernard, Bazza here. Just ringing to see if you wanna see the Sainters play on Saturday?'

Perfect. Male caller identifies himself (Bazza); 'just ringing' implies this will be a short conversation; and then straight to the point about going to the football. There is nothing superfluous in this conversation. Male social chat on the phone should henceforth be referred to as Greyhound Conversation: thin, sleek and not exactly pretty discussions designed to chase a hare conclusion.

I suspect that this male aversion to telephone chat is something that takes grip later in life. Generation Y men don't seem to have an issue with telephone chitchat. Perhaps men do not recover as well as women from the trauma of raising teenagers, because by fifty, men are dumbstruck when it comes to social chat on the phone. Consider the awkward reality of a call to the parental home by a twenty-something daughter. And Dad answers:

'Hey, Dad, how are you?'

'Fine thanks Sweetie, and you?'

'Great, Dad. I'm fine.'

'Good. Good. How's your car going?'

'Car's fine, Dad.'

'Good. Good. I'll just get your mother …'

'Hey, Mum. Can you tell Dad …'

The problem for post-fifty men is that they have a limited range of safe discussion topics—whereas women can talk on a wide range of subjects. Cars and football are good manly topics, as is traffic: 'Which way did you come? Did you come down the highway or did you take the coast road because the coast road this time of year can be busy. They really need to do something about that intersection.' The other man favourite is weather: 'Did you get any rain down your way last night? We got 20 mill. The radar looked real dark over Melbourne.' Safe, sleek topics where the conclusion is immediately apparent and which do not involve disclosure of thoughts or feelings. And that's just the way we men like it.

With more and more men pushing beyond fifty, I suspect that we will be seeing Greyhound Conversation increasingly enter the mainstream in the future. Perhaps there needs to be a website where those seeking to converse with males over fifty by telephone can get inspiration for safe topics.

The secrets of yuletide harmony

How it's really men who always save the day on Christmas Day

ABOUT three weeks prior to the day, men throughout Christendom will be asked what they think should be on the menu for Christmas lunch. Fellas, beware, for this is not only a trick question; it is a dangerous question. Do not be deluded into thinking your loving partner needs your advice about what to cook for Christmas lunch. If she needed counsel on this or any other matter, she would turn to someone with a modicum of credibility: her mother or her best girlfriend, with whom she is in daily contact. No, what women are asking when they say, 'What do you think we should have for lunch on Christmas Day?' is 'Tell me I'm doing a fantastic job organising Christmas lunch for all the rellies.'

So the appropriate response is this: 'Well, if the weather is fine we could go for seafood. But because Christmas falls on a Sunday this year, there might be a problem with freshness. Or you could go the traditional turkey. What I can say is this: I don't know how you do it.' Bing. Go. The answer must incorporate an intellectual understanding of the technical issues (delivering seafood on a Sunday) as well as an acknowledgement that a big Christmas lunch doesn't just happen. Do not, fellas, say something like 'Whatever—you choose' or 'Let's just go out for lunch.' Men simply do not get it. Go out for lunch? Go out for lunch? How would that look to the in-laws? It would look like I couldn't do it! I'll show them.

Christmas lunch isn't a mere lunch; it is a display of power and proficiency. Power is reflected in the consumer largesse that is on display: plasma telly, computer games for the kids, branded clothing, table setting with chichi white crockery. Proficiency is displayed in the scale and in the stunning deliciosity—yes, the deliciosity—of the meal. Even the table decoration must be just so; a red and green theme is de rigueur. Oh, and just to show that you are not too uptight about the day, how about some jaunty Christmas-tree earrings? Let the part-tee begin because the Christmas-tree earrings are on display. I don't know about you but I can hardly contain my excitement.

Fellas, there's something else you should know about Christmas Day. Do not presume to know what to wear. That's why women give men clothes for Christmas. Otherwise, it'd get to an hour before everyone is due to arrive and he is just as likely to walk out of the bedroom wearing, ahem, the wrong clothes. Ladies, you know exactly what I mean. Those jeans where the fly doesn't quite do up and that polo shirt that makes him look pregnant. 'Darling, why don't you put on your smart new clothes? I'm taking photos and I want you to look your best. And it's your new boat shoes, not your old boat shoes. And make sure you do your hair!'

Now of course, all of this organising of men by women around Christmas Day lunch can lead to tensions. Men can get to feeling they are being manoeuvred like a pawn in a giant chess game. Which they are, but that's beside the point. And ladies, we all know where that leads: an emasculated male hissy fit moments before the event begins. And that is why women give men jobs in the lead-up to Christmas lunch to make them feel important. Jobs such as manning the barbecue or selecting the wine and making sure the beer is really, really cold. That's men's work. It's tough. It's important. It's dangerous. Perhaps you ladies might like to step back from the vicinity of the bar fridge while we rearrange things. Yes, I might put the sauvignon blanc on top of the Cascade Light. Only men can do this. And especially men who are wearing smart new clothes and brand-new boat shoes.

Brought undone by a cheeky kiss

Social kissing can be a tricky business for men and women

YOU will have to excuse my ignorance but men are not always up with the latest fashionable behaviour, especially as it applies to greetings and goodbyes. Social mores are on the move and, as usual, I am a bit slow on the uptake. I am speaking of course of the recent phenomenon of women kissing men socially in a cosmopolitan sort of way. Not *Cosmopolitan*, as in the racy women's magazine full of tips for hot, hot … never mind, I'm sure it's a weather report. I mean cosmopolitan in a chichi, French sort of way. Air kissing—that's what I'm talkin' about.

In the old days we blokes knew where we stood. We knew the polite thing to do was to shake the hand of a woman you had just been introduced to. And of course we knew not to give a manly handshake but a girly grip-the-tips sort of handshake. Before the 1970s there was no contact in these situations at all. A male's introduction to a female required no more than delivery of an earnest nod. And the more the male wished to impress, the more pronounced the nod. In fact this nod was really a bit of a jerk. Off would go the head nodding up and nodding down.

But this protocol has been turned on its head by the advent of what can be described only as a kissing epidemic. Australian women have caught on to the European affectation of kissing hello and goodbye. And pretty much everyone in a social circle is likely to cop a kiss. Now we blokes don't mind a bit of air kissing, but we do need to know the rules: who intends air kissing and who doesn't. I have been at functions where I have shaken hands with a female dining companion at the beginning of a dinner but by the goodbye she's up for a full-on air kiss. But we only ate together. That's not grounds for a relationship transition from handshake to air kiss, is it? My dinner conversation wasn't that sparkling, was it? Then again maybe it was. I did regale her with several amusing observations about the most recent edition of *Australian Demographic Quarterly*.

When is it appropriate to air kiss and when is it appropriate to shake hands? Sometimes it's obvious; sometimes it's not. How about when you are one of three men meeting a woman who already knows the other two? She will of course greet them with an air kiss, but what does she do when she comes to you? It can look as if you're lining up for a kiss when in fact you've never met. It can look as if you are trying to fraudulently create a kiss situation simply by association. No, I am not expecting a kiss; I just happen to be in the vicinity of blokes who you seem to know. I have found that in such circumstances women usually dole out a kiss to the third man on the basis that if you are a friend of her friends, then you are probably air kiss–worthy.

But the protocol problems for men don't end there. Is it just one kiss or is it two? In Paris it's two; in lusty Provence it's three. Now this multiple kissing business can lead to some mighty tricky situations. What if the woman whom you are about to greet is clearly expecting an air kiss, so you manoeuvre your preferred cheek into the classic kiss-receptive position? Ahh, that's all very well, but what happens when you think there's only one air kiss and the woman does the Paris thing and heads for your other cheek for a second kiss? You don't realise what she's doing, so you straighten up, and as she passes your mouth en route to the other cheek, your lips and her lips collide. Yes. I am talking about the Accidental Lip Kiss. This would never happen if there were clear rules and protocols. One kiss is fine, but if you are intending a two-kiss move, then, ladies, please signal your intent with a 'two-please' statement on approach. That way both men and women know exactly where they stand on the protocol of air kissing hello and goodbye.

What's the French for Clump?

New terms are needed to define our newest relationships

THERE are times when modern behaviour races ahead of modern language. What, for example, do you call the partner of your gay son or daughter? Boyfriend or girl-friend seems a tad twee. And until gay marriage is legalised (which surely can't be too far away), I don't see how *son-* or *daughter-in-law* can legitimately be used. I have never liked the term *partner* to describe an intimate other. Hmmm, what do you think about *Intimate Other*? The problem here is that the basis of the relationship, intimacy, is front and centre. Although when you think about it, no one worries about being introduced as a workmate, which also show-cases the basis of the relationship. Somehow I cannot see the term *bedmate* ever getting currency. And *lover* is just so completely in your face. That cute French couple *fiancé* and *fiancée* require commitment but, in fact, many modern cohabiting couples may not be committed. There they are wafting along in a temporal state of romantic bliss. Sigh.

In the past such couples have been either boyfriend or girlfriend or they were betrothed; there was nothing in between. Not so today. A range of relationships have blossomed on the fertile savannah that stretches between the school formal (the new debutante ball) and marriage (late twenties to early thirties). And I am not talking about one-night stands and illicit affairs. After all, I have it on very good authority that lust and licentiousness have been around for some time and are likely to remain popular institutions for decades to come. However, while I'm on this subject, why is it that the French so dominate this perhaps flawed aspect of the human condition? French words such as *affair*, *dilettante*, *roué*, *paramour* and *libertine* as well as a number of other blush-worthy concepts suggest this nationality has had a greater than usual need to get a very firm grip on such matters. *C'est la vie*, I suppose.

And so to the issue. What we need is a new term to describe young couples who live together and who, let's be frank, sleep together but who acknowledge that the relationship may or may not proceed to a formal and committed union. As is often the case in popular demography, I have found a solution in an acronym. How about cohabiting lovers uncommitted to marriage or partnership, or Clump? The beauty of *Clump* is that it is versatile and so can be used to describe a straight or gay relationship or indeed any one of the parties within that relationship. 'Hello I'd like you to meet my son and his Clump.' Or, 'My daughter is in a lovely Clump relationship in Sydney.' Perfect. In one fell swoop you have transmitted the fact that a special relationship exists between the parties but through the use of an acronym the telltale term *lover* is coquettishly shielded from public scrutiny. *Coquettish*, isn't that a French word? *Mon Dieu* the French have been active in this arena. Or is it that the English have been so unimaginative when it comes to the language of love that they have had to borrow the lot from across the Channel?

Please consider *Clump*: it's subtle, it's new and it boldly goes where no satisfactory term has gone before. Clearly *Clump* is the Starship *Enterprise* of the demographic world: its purpose is to explore and chart new territory. The only thing holding *Clump* back from the stardom it so richly deserves is its unfortunate phonetics. *Clump* has the misfortune to rhyme with *rump*, *dump*, *stump* and *chump*. I am sure the stylish gay community would never have a thing to do with a drab-sounding word like *Clump* for this very reason. That is of course unless I give it a cunning and exotic makeover. Let's turn *Clump* from an ugly duckling into a beautiful swan. How about Frenchifying the term to *Clumpé* for males and to *Clumpée* for females. *Magnifique, n'est-ce pas?*

Big day out, bonding over bargains

Going clothes shopping is a crucial social and family event for most women

YOU will appreciate this is a brave column for a man to write. Or indeed a foolish column for a man to write. And that's because it deals with women and their shopping habits. Through the years I have made a study of Clothes Shopping Women and their behaviours. And now it's time for me to impart to the next generation what I have learnt, often painfully and by trial and error.

Perhaps it's because women traditionally have been food collectors and preparers that they are comfortable with all the bartering that goes on in the marketplace. I'm not sure whether you've noticed this too, but I think men are different when it comes to clothes shopping. Typically a man's aim is to get in and out of a shop with a minimum of engagement. Women, on the other hand, seem to have no trouble walking into a shop, looking at every rack, trying things on, getting the sales assistant to help them try things on and then—get this—walking out of the shop without making a commitment. How do they do that? Saying, 'I'll think about it' to a shop assistant is the same as saying 'No, thank you'; the shop assistant knows you won't be back; they probably think that you're nothing but a sales tease.

I have a confession. I often feel sorry for the sales assistant who probably hasn't sold anything all day, so I do my best to find something I like. Why do I secretly want the approval of a sales assistant whom I have never met and will never meet again? Is this a male thing? Or is this a me thing? And so it is for this very reason that some men—not saying anyone in particular—can never be trusted to shop alone for clothes. Fellas, how many jeans do you own? How many do you actually wear? Enough said.

Do you know how women like to shop? Not for food but for clothes or shoes or soft furnishings or gifts or anything other than the day-to-day? They like to shop with other women. The most potent combination of Clothes Shopping Women is, in my vast experience, best friends. Or, better still, women and their daughters or women and their mothers. Up to the mid-forties, women love to clothes shop with their mother or their girlfriends; after the mid-forties, teenage daughters make their appearance as shopping companions and critics: 'No, Mum, you can't wear that. Mum, put it back. Mum!'

The reason these combinations of women make good shopping companions is because they know each other's wardrobe. Now you probably think I mean they know some items from each other's wardrobe. No. I mean they know each other's wardrobes to the point that if something new appears, they know that it's new. Indeed they will say, 'That's new; where did you get it? How much was it?' And if there is a particularly close relationship between the Clothes Shopping Women, the person with the new item will say she got it from David Jones on sale and with a flourish add that it was originally $200 but she got it for $120. And at this point the woman who asked how much it was is required to exclaim that she has 'done well'.

There is another part of the day that Clothes Shopping Women especially enjoy. It is not the shopping, the trying on, the afternoon cuppa to discuss husbands/boyfriends/ life with daughter/mother/best friend; it is the post-shop show and tell. This is where men have a part to play. Men are instructed to sit while new things are paraded before them. The required response from the man is something along the lines of 'Hmmm, that looks nice.' Now there's a trap here. At some point the man will be asked what he thinks such and such cost. Do not underestimate. Go over- board. Go high. Go really high. Say, 'I bet that cost $500.' To which Clothes Shopping Woman will say: 'Ha. No way. I got it for $75, on sale.'

After the man has said the right things, he is dispensed with and Clothes Shopping Women then get on with the business of clothes trading: 'My new dress will look good with your new shoes.' And therein lies the story and the behaviour of Clothes Shopping Women. It has nothing to do with shopping; it is a familial and socially bonding experience that affirms relationships with other supportive women. That's why women like to shop for clothes with other women.

The tyranny of distance makes love a foreign affair for some

With their fondness for travel, Aussies and Kiwis are prone to long-distance relationships

I CANNOT prove what I am about to assert but that does not mean that the phenomenon doesn't exist. I think that cultures like Australia, and New Zealand for that matter, are more likely to support long-distance relationships (or LDRs) than just about anywhere else. And by LDRs I mean long-distance intimate relationships.

'How can this be?' I hear you ask. Easily, I reply. Australia and New Zealand have a culture of young people travelling overseas. We call it a gap year; the Kiwis call it their 'OE', meaning their overseas experience. The logic is that because we are both so cut off from the northern-hemisphere centres of business and culture, we colonials feel compelled to spend part of our youth in London or New York or wherever, just so long as it's a bit exciting.

Work by demographer Graeme Hugo a few years ago on Australian expatriates concluded that after four years young Aussies tend to 'go native', which means they end up staying. After five years an Australian abroad is likely to have established a relationship with a local and/ or they have progressed sufficiently in an organisation that it becomes difficult to get a similar position back in Australia. Plus after four years their Australian friendship and job-contact networks are likely to have cooled. The lesson for parents is this: if your son or daughter is gapping in London, you really want to get them back within four years. Otherwise you might be damned to forever visit your grandchildren abroad.

The other scenario is that the young Aussie abroad meets an attractive local or, more problematically, another colonial from another part of the empire (other than New Zealand) and strikes up a relationship. Imagine, for example, the ramifications of a Perth boy meeting a Saskatchewan girl in London where they become a passionate and inseparable item. Gap year ends; each returns to their respective countries, but the relationship refuses to end. Phone calls, emails, texts, visits here and visits there. Weeks and months pass and still this logistically flawed relationship refuses to die. What to do? Well-meaning parents offer helpful observations: 'Why do you insist on pursuing difficult relationships? Dump the Canadian/Australian. There are plenty of local candidates worthy of your affection.'

But such is the delicious frisson and the impossible folly of LDRs that no amount of counselling by third parties can end the dream. Do you think some people are gluttons for punishment when it comes to cultivating difficult relationships? Do you think some people like the martyrdom of the perennially unsated love that so marks the LDR? What are the benefits? Perhaps the all too brief encounters are outstandingly electric because of periods of enforced restraint.

I also wonder whether given normal circumstances—that is daily contact—both parties might not otherwise establish pretty quickly that actually they're not that well suited. After all, to be engaged in an LDR is to be engaged in a permanent honeymoon. You need time together to get sick of each other and so with only fleeting 'meet' times the relationship may well be held for months in a state of suspended animation. During World War II many such relationships existed for years on end with only the occasional letter to sustain interest. Today with Skype and email and even cheap telephone connectivity combined with more young people travelling abroad, surely the scope for LDR formation is greater than ever.

What I want to know is whether an LDR is stronger, lasts longer and is more intense because both parties have had to mutually fight for its existence? I also wonder whether the indulged children of indulgent parents are naturally drawn to the drama of being committed to an unattainable lover? Will we find, though, that the famous impatience of gen Ys means that they do not have the self-sacrificing predisposition that is needed to make a long-distance relationship work? I suspect that LDRs are on the rise and especially in colonial outposts such as Australia and New Zealand.

The Man Flu Conspiracy Pact

Men don't get sick; they have a brush with death

HOW was my holiday? Well. If you must know, I was sick. Really sick. I caught some exotic bug on a plane and promptly contracted a chronic lung infection. I had a temperature and I couldn't breathe. I went to my local GP and she said, 'Bernard, this is the worst case of chronic lung infection I have ever seen.' She said she was so concerned that she wanted me to be ready to be rushed to hospital at a moment's notice. Okay, so she didn't say exactly that but I could tell she was thinking exactly that. I could see it in her eyes. They sort of narrowed when I told her my symptoms: fever, runny nose, aching. I've seen that look before on doctors' faces on TV: it's the he's-got-something-terminal-but-I-can't-tell-him-just-yet look.

You will appreciate that I am never sick. I have always enjoyed rude health. Which is why being laid up with a life-threatening lung infection was so traumatic. But I didn't want to cause a fuss. I never like to cause a fuss. Just a cup of tea and a bit of a lie down. No. No. No. Don't alter your plans. If it gets any worse, I'll bite the doona; it stifles the pain. You see that's the sort of person—man, really—I am: fearless when it comes to personal discomfort. Thank you. I agree. I am selfless. Unfortunately not everyone has your level of emotional maturity.

And what thanks did I get for being brave? None. Not a sausage. In fact do you know what some people—some *female* people—said to me? They said, 'Bernard, you are suffering from nothing more than a bad case of Man Flu.' You do know Man Flu don't you? This is the fantastical concept that if a woman gets a cold then it's a cold but if a man gets a cold then it's the flu. Thank you. I agree. Man Flu is a sexist and baseless concept. My illness was different. I didn't have a cold. I didn't have the flu. I didn't even have a lung infection. I had a chronic lung infection. A chronic lung infection is three notches up on the Sick Scale from a cold. I could have died. Died! But thankfully I pulled through the first twenty-four hours.

On the second day of my illness I was so concerned that the antibiotics weren't working, that I was deteriorating and that I was minutes from being rushed to hospital that I went back to my GP. I said I was burning up. I said the fire within was now a raging inferno. I said I wanted the last rites. I said I had said goodbye to the children. She said, 'Bernard, I'll take your temperature.' And then do you know what she said? She said, 'Oh good, you're down from 38 yesterday to 37 today.'

Excuse me, Ms GP, but I am burning up here and you're telling me I'm getting better? You're telling me that all my agonising and all my flailing about over the last few hours have been for nought but dramatic effect? Well don't you go thinking that I haven't worked you out, Ms GP. I bet you're a signatory to the Man Flu Conspiracy Pact, an evil charter designed to promote the idea that men are prone to exaggerate symptoms when they get sick. Well I'll be taking this matter further, Ms GP, much further, assuming of course that I ever pull out of this chronic-lung-infection death spiral.

9

Time and Tide

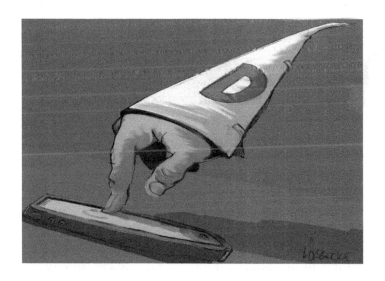

MAYBE it's a matter of getting older but many of the matters that occupy the mind later in life involve comparisons with our experiences earlier in life. There was a time when new technology came and was mastered by all—the video recorder and the answering machine, for example. But today the pace of technological change is constant. New phones have new features, to say nothing of new personal security numbers and protocols for logging in to everything from work emails to bank accounts. Now it's possible that many people love nothing more than clogging up their available brain space with learning how to operate new gadgetry. But then there are others, like me, who would rather allocate that brain space to other activities and so find shortcuts around the new arrangements. But accommodating new technology is just part of the minutiae of modern life. There are mental comparisons to be made about how and what we eat today compared with back then. Then there's the question of what relationship with a commercial product has remained with you the longest. For me it is a brand of toothpaste and toothbrush. Others might muse about how personal relationships have changed and indeed how life has changed. Much of what matters in the minds of those in, say, the last third of the life cycle is not so much what happened years ago but how things today compare with how things were.

Tech rules, but not in my car

Not everyone likes to keep up with the latest technology

I HAVE a confession that I suspect will upset some people. Until recently I didn't know how to put telephone numbers into my iPhone directory. I know, I know. I'm supposed to be a smart person and I am. No, really, I am. I have two degrees. I have written four popular books. I write this column. (Okay, so this column isn't proof of anything other than an ability to chat about the unchattable.) It's just that I have these 'blind spots' when it comes to mastering everyday technology. Although, as I get older and as household technology changes, my blind spots are coalescing into a blackout.

It started thirty-five years ago when I bought my first calculator. I only ever used the plus, minus, multiply and divide buttons. I never mastered the square root key; it was a level of mathematical sophistication that was superfluous to my needs. Same thing with alarm clocks. In the old days, clocks ticked by beds; the alarm was set by shifting a hand and by flicking a switch to 'on'. Then in the 1980s alarm clocks got all techno-uppity and went electronic. Red glowing numbers at night were a sign that a technological wizard slept nearby. The problem was that the electronic clock's operation was never consistent between manufacturers. Clocks in hotel rooms went electronic at this time, no doubt in order to keep abreast of the times. But who has the inclination to work out how to set the alarm on an electronic clock in a hotel that you will move on from the next day?

Today five-star hotels have simple clocks with hands and an alarm 'on' switch. Here is clear evidence that the modern era's technological surge is being pushed back by

opposing Luddite forces. We live life at such a pace, interacting with bits and pieces of technology, that many don't
have the time or the inclination to learn how everything
works. That's why I will never learn how to adjust the clock
above the oven in my home. Or indeed the clock in my
car, which was bought pre–daylight saving. Instead I have
learnt how to manoeuvre around, and to manage the con-
sequences of, not quite mastering all aspects of everyday
technology. Get in my car and you must subtract an hour
from the dashboard clock until daylight saving ends. Is that
really so hard? It's easier to do that than find the manual
and learn how to make this adjustment twice a year.

I bought my current watch in 1997; it has hands and
a date dial. I am quite sure that TAG Heuer would have
thought of a way to progress the date at the end of short
months. But in twelve years I have never bothered to
find out. As for consulting an instruction manual, are you
crazy? We men don't do instruction manuals. Instruction
manuals, like asking someone for street directions, are for
sissies and girls. My way around this conundrum is to man-
ually wind the watch hands through 24 hours to progress
the date. And I've been doing that for a decade and a half.

In the modern world we are increasingly required to learn
and recall new technologies, processes and passwords. And
for many I am sure these changes are merely evidence of
this century's exciting world. But to others, well me, they're
yet more things that I just can't be fagged learning. I'll get by
without knowing how to conference call. I'll get by without
having your number in my directory. I just scroll through
previous calls and associate telephone numbers with individual people. Now here's the odd thing. Which do you think
takes more effort: spending five minutes learning how to put

phone numbers into a directory, or learning how to associate a phone number with an individual? Logic tells us that we should embrace and learn the new technologies, but somehow and for some reason we revert to all sorts of manoeuvrings in order to avoid the realities of technological change.

Perhaps making new technology Luddite-friendly is as much a challenge for today's hi-tech companies as is coming up with breakthrough technologies.

Vegging out on memories

Did bok choy exist in the 1960s, and if so, where was it hiding?

WHEN I was a kid growing up in the 1960s, meals were simple. Chops, potatoes, carrots and peas. And on a Sunday there would be a roast, which we ate at lunchtime and called dinner. Dinner was called tea. I might also add that dessert was called pudding, regardless of whether it was an actual pudding or pavlova or fruit salad. Pudding always followed roast. We drank tea not coffee, although by the early 70s the smart set drank coffee. And the coffee of choice was powdered (Pablo brand), although this quickly upscaled into granules (via Maxwell House) and then on to the ultimate coffee experience: International Roast. I had not heard of pizza or lasagne until my late teens, although I do recall eating spaghetti, which was heated from a can. I quite liked it.

I still recall being shocked at the age of eighteen to learn that there was a vegetable called a zucchini. I put it down to the Mediterranean invasion, which by the mid-70s was influencing our palate. Where had the zucchini been hiding during my childhood? I naively assumed that the fruit and vegetable kingdom had been fully discovered. Spanish explorers found the tomato hiding somewhere deep in South America, right? And the Portuguese discovered the tea plant somewhere in China, and then introduced it to the English. But how is it the zucchini could have avoided discovery for so long? But the new vegetable revelations didn't stop there. I was unaware that the lettuce of my childhood had a name (iceberg) or indeed that there were other forms of lettuce: mesculin, cos and butter. Or that there was a spicy competitor to lettuce called arugula. I also didn't know that the salad of my childhood had a name ('garden') or that other forms of salad were even conceivable. A salad was a salad; it had lettuce, tomato, red onion, shredded carrot and a sliced boiled egg on top. And it was eaten with mayonnaise.

Bok choy emerged from I know not where in the late 90s and since then it has been joined by pak choy and choy sum. Potatoes can now be purple; others are orange and sweet. Broccoli also seemed to surface in the late 90s but then in the following decade a variation arrived known as broccolini, which I understand to be a different cultivar rather than (as I first thought) merely a baby version of grown-up broccoli. This of course brings me to the babyfication movement in the vegetable world. There are baby peas, baby carrots, baby spinach and no doubt other baby vegetables. Fruit seems to have remained more or less fruit for several decades, although different varieties have come and gone. I sort of knew as a kid that apples came as Jonathan, Granny Smith and Golden Delicious. But Pink Lady and Fuji? Are these new inventions, or like the zucchini, is it that we just weren't looking in the right places?

Do not get me started on beverages. Okay, you asked for it. Tea. Apparently the tea I was drinking as a kid was black tea. Not that it was important to qualify tea back then because there was no other kind. But as coffee morphed from the heady heights of International Roast to cappuccino then on to latte, espresso and macchiato, the tea fraternity clearly decided to match coffee's splinterfication by introducing green tea, white tea and chai tea.

I sometimes wonder whether the children of today will look back from the altitude of 2050 and marvel at the culinary naivety of the society in which they grew up.

Everything old can be used again

Necessity isn't the mother of invention; it's the mother of sustainability

WHEN I was growing up in the 1960s we had a metal container in one of the kitchen cupboards that we called 'the string tin'. And do you know what we kept in the string tin? String. That's right, my frugal mother saved string. That's what you did if you went through the Great Depression as a kid and through wartime rationing as a newlywed: you saved stuff. I am somewhat ashamed to say that in my own household today we have a cavalier attitude towards string. I am so rich that whenever I want string I think nothing of buying it at the supermarket. You know how Scrooge McDuck dives into a swimming pool of money—okay, so maybe you don't know, but my research suggests that he does—well, baby boomer kids such as myself dream about diving into a pool of string.

Not only did our household save string but we also saved the tops of Lan-Choo tea packets, which could be redeemed for tea towels. Tea towels. For free. Do you know that if my household needs tea towels today we go to a shop and we buy new ones. As many as we like. I have a confession. When we renovated our kitchen some years ago we threw out several perfectly good tea towels and bought a set 'that fitted the new colour scheme'. It's very important in the modern world to have tea towels that don't clash with the crockery or cabinetry. In my aspirational swimming pool of string, there will be a deep end of tea towels.

But the thrift DNA of the Depression generation goes further than a penchant for string and tea towels. By the 1970s the packaging of butter transitioned from grease-proof wrapper to 'plastic container with detachable lid'. Well, you can guess what my frugal mother did with all those containers: she washed, dried and stacked the lot in the garage. Why? Because they might come in handy one day, silly. And do you know those containers are still there. Like the silent terracotta warriors of Xian, they await the day of their glorious resurrection when they will be transformed into, oh I don't know, a container for Anzac biscuits to give to the grandchildren.

The problem is that the rate of resurrection is slower than the rate of saving. So the saved containers grow like leaning towers of Pisa yearning for another chance at life. And when these containers do get to my place and the Anzac biscuits are demolished, the container is blithely thrown into the recyclables. As I drop the container into the bin, the whole process seems so wrong: that a container that has been lovingly saved for years by a Frugal should be discarded after a single use by a boomer. The same goes for today's abundance of string and tea towels: consumer goods come and go all too easily for the postwar generations.

Although I will say there is one aspect of the frugal kitchen that has survived the decades. In the drawers below the string tin, near the tea towel drawer, there was, and I suspect there remains in every kitchen today, a drawer known only as 'the junk drawer'. The string tin might be disappearing, as is the abomination of mismatched tea towels, but there will always be a need for a junk drawer. In fact not only has the junk drawer survived the decades but it has metamorphosed. Indeed it is no longer a drawer; it has supersized and now commandeers an entire room and is making moves on the garage. And do you know why we need a junk room today instead of just a junk drawer? It's because we own more stuff despite the fact that we also discard more stuff. Isn't that funny? Here we are: the most green-conscious generation in history and yet our conservation efforts are still being topped by the money-saving habits of the fast-fading Frugals.

Flashbacks from the land before time

Life was primitive, but we didn't know and didn't care

COME with me to a time and place from whence many have come but about which few have spoken. I want to talk about the land before time, a time when beds had but a single pillow and when black-and-white television broadcast a test pattern. I want to talk about the minutiae of life in Australian suburbia in the 1960s.

Here was a time when fast food meant fish and chips, when clocks and watches ticked, when the national anthem was played in cinemas and when spanking children in public was regarded as a sign of good parenting. This was a time before ice-cream commandeered the refrigerator freezer box and when a treat was white bread spread with full-fat butter and sprinkled with sugary hundreds and thousands. This was a time when everyone drank Robur or Lan-Choo tea and the only variations were with or without milk and with or without sugar.

Let me speak of a time when men rolled their own ciga-rettes and when a good hostess dutifully fetched an ashtray should a guest decide to light up at the table. Let me speak of a time when the young baby boomersaurus roamed the suburban savannah gambolling and frolicking with gay (meaning happy) abandon, unrestrained and unsupervised on busy streets. Let me take you back a half century to what life was like before we became sophisticated.

I first heard of the term *pizza* as a teenager in 1974. I did not know what lasagne was until 1981. I discovered the zucchini only in the late 80s. That zucchinis had flowers and that these flowers could be eaten was a later, more shocking revelation. As a kid I thought cheese came wrapped in foil in a blue cardboard packet. It didn't occur to me that was more than one kind of lettuce. Why would God make multiples of lettuce? That would be doubling up; surely God has better things to do than muck around creating umpteen varieties of lettuce. It didn't occur to me that daggy, dirty beetroot could be cool or that it could be combined with pastry and topped with goat's cheese to form a tart. I hadn't heard of bok choy until 1998.

I remember when the toilet was known as the lavatory. Interestingly, with the arrival of reticulated sewerage, the outdoor English lav became all uppity and Frenchified and rebranded itself as the indoor toilet. And it was in the late 60s that tissues usurped handkerchiefs as the preferred method of blowing one's nose. My Depression-raised parents were aghast at the waste: some people were so well-to-do that they could blow their nose on disposable paper! What was wrong with a handkerchief? Not that we had handkerchiefs. An old cotton sheet cut into squares and hemmed on a treadle sewing machine did the trick.

Holidays were spent at the beach in a caravan or in a beach hut that was an unplumbed, unwired and, most likely, illegally constructed shack. Vegetables were grown in the backyard not because of some earth-mother, save-the-planet schtick but to save money. Chooks were also kept in the backyard. At Christmas Dad would take a chook over to the woodheap and chop off its head with an axe in front of his six children and a couple of the neighbour's kids hanging over the fence.

There was church on Sunday mornings, after which we would stop off at a milk bar to buy cream to put on the pavlova that followed the lamb roast. This meal was known as dinner; dinner, on the other hand, was called tea; no one did lunch and no one other than relatives ever joined the family for a meal. No one knew anyone who had been overseas; Bali didn't surface in our consciousness until the late 70s—although in 1968 my older brother went from Melbourne to Surfers Paradise on a plane and came back with a golden tan. He said there were no clocks in Surfers. We were agog with the exotica of a land without clocks in the land before time.

Innocent as charged

Learning the correct way to throw a bottle from a moving vehicle

WHEN I was a kid in the early 1960s our family had a black, late-1940s Chevrolet that Dad would drive to various destinations—usually relatives—in country Victoria. Mum, Dad and six kids aged three to twelve would pile onto the front and back leather bench seats. The mandatory use of seatbelts was still a decade away. Being the second youngest, I was always squeezed between Mum and Dad in the front. Mum nursed my younger sister. I am sure that that car never travelled faster than 80 kilometres per hour, but when it braked Dad would put his left hand out to stop me being carried forward into the dashboard. Mum simply clasped my sister more tightly and pressed her feet into the floor. Who needed seatbelts? No one viewed this as reckless practice. In fact Dad probably thought he was exercising due parental care by holding me back.

My point is that the way we see the world on a range of behavioural matters changed profoundly later in the century and will continue to change in the future. I wonder what we are doing now that will prompt Australians of the 2060s to reel back in horror.

There is a scene from *Mad Men* set in the unenlightened 1960s where main characters Don and Betty Draper and their children get up from a picnic rug in an idyllic rural setting and simply leave their litter on the ground. The idea that littering might be regarded as a crime against the planet was, like the mandatory wearing of seatbelts, years into the future.

In the same vein I again recall from country car trips at around this time my father explaining the correct way to throw a bottle from a moving vehicle. It should never be thrown from the passenger window: the slipstream invariably draws it back onto the road where it might be a hazard to oncoming traffic. No. The correct way to throw a bottle from a moving vehicle is for the driver to lob it up and over the top of the vehicle and into the verge beyond thereby avoiding the slipstream altogether. We were agog; Dad was right; there is a right way to throw a bottle from a moving vehicle.

At school there were everyday occurrences that would now cause offence or present as an unacceptable risk. At my primary school, the Sisters of Mercy—whom I adored, I might add—maintained strict control through liberal use of the strap. This was a piece of brown leather cowhide say 70 millimetres wide by 300 millimetres long that was neatly finished with cream stitching. It is only now, later in life, that I wonder: Was the strap a standard product issued to schools? Or did my primary school put in a special request to the local bootmaker? And if it was especially made, how would such a request have been phrased by the principal?

'Would you mind making me a strap so that I might flog children at the school?'

'Certainly. Would you like the light or dark stitching?'

The schoolyard contained steel playground equipment including a contraption known as monkey bars, which was a kind of ladder that ran parallel to but perhaps two metres above the ground. It seemed to me that every week one kid fell from the monkey bars and broke their arm or leg. Rubberised matting, opportunistic litigation and risk-mitigation signage were all at that time yet to be invented.

I wonder what sensitivities, what correctness, what behavioural prescriptions might emerge by the middle of the century? What? You mean there were places called butcher shops that displayed the carcasses of butchered animals in the window? Do you mean to tell me that 80 000 random, unscreened people would gather weekly at the MCG and not one thought it might be a good idea to wear a surgical mask? Really? How could the people of the 2010s have been so naive, so unthinking, so childlike in their view of the world?

Dentally devoted to a fault

Some relationships stay with you for life

WHAT is the longest relationship you have had in your life? Apart from your mother and father and siblings, that is. They don't count because in this exercise I am only interested in relationships of choice. Who or what have you chosen to be in your life for the longest unbroken length of time? Your partner? Well, for many people partners seem to come and go with the greatest of ease. As for lovers, well, are these not trial partners? If partners in the modern world are fleeting, then lovers must be even more fleeting.

But my quest to find examples of long-term relationships is not confined to the intimate world. For example, I have followed the St Kilda Football Club for forty-five years. That's right, since before I was born. It is a relationship that, no matter how frustrated I get, I simply cannot break. Is this love? I have heard that some people change football-team allegiance each year, depending on performance. I have one word to describe these people: flibbertigibbets.

Is there anything regularly in your life now that was also there when you were, say, at primary school? For some this might be religious belief, perhaps. Others might say that their values haven't changed: that they still adhere to the same moral code of honesty and integrity. But what I have in mind is something from the material world. What I am thinking of is toothpaste. I cannot think of any other thing or item of clothing or jewellery or possession that has stayed the course of my life, from childhood to what is now middle age, other than toothpaste. And here's the thing: I am brand loyal to Colgate. I have no idea how many toothpaste brands there are, but what I do know is that the toothpaste aisle extends forever. There is so much choice that I cannot make a choice other than the brand that I have always known.

But my brand allegiance peculiarities do not exactly end there. I am also brand loyal to a particular type of toothbrush: I buy Tek toothbrushes. You probably haven't heard of Tek; they're old-fashioned and—sorry, Tek management—they're also a bit daggy. No bells and whistles; in fact, very plain. Suits my personality perfectly, don't you think? The other thing about Tek is that they come in soft, medium and hard. Only sissies buy soft-bristled toothbrushes. You need hard, man-like bristles to get off all that plaque and tartar that I have seen in toothpaste advertisements. However, Tek brushes are hard to find, so when I do come across a supermarket that stocks this brand, I frantically stockpile. If there is a nuclear war and I am bunkered down for years, I have a personal supply of Tek toothbrushes that will see me through to 2030. And I'm not sharing with anyone.

I have no idea why I am brand loyal to St Kilda, to Colgate and to Tek, but these are the sorts of deep psychological relationships that send marketing people into a frenzy of pleasure. I wonder whether, in an increasingly temporal world where intimate, personal and professional relationships come and go, there is a need for stability that is now being met through brand loyalty. After all, even flighty, flaky, flibbertigibbety generation Y does seem to have an unhealthy fixation on Apple technology. Is it possible for some brands to become the rock, the stable force, the replacement lovers—yes, you heard me, replacement lovers—in the lives of modern consumers whose real-world lives seem to be in constant turmoil?

Wedding lists: a fresh idea

There may be something in the concept of arranged marriages

YOU know there comes a point in every parent's life, usually in the late forties or early fifties, when their thoughts turn to marriage. Not their own marriage. No. No. No. Their own marriages are fine, thank you very much. Middle-aged parents wake up one day and start thinking of their children's marriages. Or, to be more precise, about their children's permanent partner selection, which in the normal course of events leads to marriage.

It's funny, but the older some parents get, the more they start to think that there might just be something in the concept of arranged marriages. Now don't get all het up about this. I'm just floating the idea. Permanent partner commitment is a big step and, well, is this really best left to the young and the inexperienced? Relationship attraction is a little bit like crème brûlée—stay with me on this—all delicious and crusty and glistening on top, but soon enough cracks start to appear and underneath there lurks a soft and gooey subterranean substance that is completely different from what's happening on top. Does anyone else think of these things when they eat crème brûlée? That it presents as one thing but in reality it's something different? Cheater dessert.

Now, as you know, I am not an unreasonable person, so my idea of a thoroughly modern incarnation of a thoroughly ancient practice would be to offer children of marriageable age a list. Any name on the list would be fine. Parents don't mind. All names would be vetted; that's the beauty. Vetted, I hear you say? Yes, vetted. To vet. To check out. To ensure that prospective permanent partner material is, well, suitable. Good home. Nice family. Respectful. Parents who are, gosh, remarkably just like us.

Although I suspect that some parents would take things too far and place an asterisk against some names to suggest, for example, that this one has particularly good prospects. Why is it that some people must always take things too far and spoil it for everyone else? There should be no asterisks on The List of Prospective Partners. Why, the very idea is a complete abomination. Now of course if some names happen to be at the top of the list and bolded and in a bigger point size, then that's completely different. That's just happenstance.

Now I'm going to let you in on a secret. I am actually a very intuitive person. I sense things. And I sense that generation Y may not take the idea of a list of prospective partners seriously. They might in fact get all antsy and suggest all manner of things that could be done with just such a list. And that is why middle-aged parents must band together to secretly communicate about who may and who may not be on the list that dare not speak its name. Code words must be used: 'Hmmm, he does seem like a nice boy' translates as 'He's on the list.' But middle-aged parents must be eternally vigilant so that they do not tip off generation Y as to the list manipulation that is actually going on: nonchalance is the key. Or, to be precise, the perception of nonchalance. And all of this is necessary to ensure that no crème brûlée candidates make it through to the final round of permanent partner selection.

Look, it's just an idea. It's a bit out there. It may not be for everyone. But somehow I suspect that when every parent looks deep inside, there is a list of prospective partners that is just waiting to be exposed to the world. It's all a question of the degree to which that list makes its way from a loose collection of thoughts into an articulated reality. I'm sensing that it's probably best to leave the list as a loose collection of thoughts. At this stage.

Goodbye 'burbs, I'm trending up

Time to get into the groove of the hipster lifestyle

I'M sick of being boring and suburban. I have decided to groove it up by converting to the church of inner-city trendism. Out goes my wardrobe of chinos, boat shoes and polo shirts, the uniform of the professional urban middle class in nice suburbs. In comes black jeans, black shirt and black suede shoes. As well as an obscure European brand of watch with a huge face. How do you think I'd go with a tattoo? I'm thinking a Chinese character on my forearm. Mandatory I'm afraid if you want to become part of the inner-city set. Same goes for an ear stud (diamond preferred) or, ideally but not absolutely de rigueur, either an eyebrow or a nose ring. And if you cannot contemplate the pain of any of these options then you simply must have a thumb ring. Yes, a thumb ring. I mean how on earth is anyone going to know that you are really, really trendy if you are only relying on them catching a glimpse of your obscure branded watch? The solution of course is to sport a silver thumb ring. Yes, silver. Look, I don't know why it has to be silver, it just has to be, all right? Sheesh, you suburbanites really have no idea, do you?

As for trendy inner-city occupations, well, anything in the arts, the media, computing (extra points for web-page design) or the entertainment industry is fine. Although if you really want to make it to high society in the inner city, and frankly who doesn't, then you need to work for an environmental cause that can be local, national or international. Anything to do with the Amazon is well regarded.

In your spare time you can either be writing a novel or blogging about food. Here is where inner-city trendies do their best work. To be part of this set, you need to understand not just the latest restaurants and cafés, but also the pedigree of their fashionable chefs. 'Yes, well I was in Café X last week. The chef there used to be at Café Y. He moved across last year because he had a dispute with the owner and I have to say that his smashed avocado with roasted mushrooms is to die for.' Brilliant. You have demonstrated in one fell swoop that you are familiar with multiple food establishments, that you have a sophisticated culinary palate and that you know who's who. Best of all, you get to use a term like smashed avocado in public.

This is just the tip of the inner-city trendism iceberg. For men there is a complicated range of hair options to navigate: the beard-stubble look, the goatee, the tuft of hair below the bottom lip and, making a welcome comeback, long thin and pointy sideboards. Young men's hair should be coiffed to form an impressively erect crest or, if the chap is older and balding, it should be shaved off altogether. And if this is the case, then the stark bald head should be softened with rectangular, black-rimmed glasses. Hairstyles not to wear in the inner city include the mullet and the comb-over. Sport either in the cafes of Sydney's Surry Hills, Melbourne's Carlton or Brisbane's Paddington and you will be branded a philistine or, worse, a suburbanist.

There is of course a range of accoutrements required to support any claim to being an inner-city trendy. A bicycle on the veranda is good even if it isn't used. Cars should be small and European. A Toyota Prius is acceptable but only if decorated with, say, an 'Obama 08' sticker. Holidays should be taken frequently, but never to middle-class destinations such as Noosa or Fiji. Do not embarrass yourself by mentioning that you have been to the worlds on the Gold Coast. If an inner-city trendy must go to the beach, it should be an untrammelled island off the coast of Vietnam or Lombok, accessible only by fishing boat. I also hear that Berlin is favoured this year but only if you can cite the suburb in which you stayed (hint: Prenzlauer Berg beats Potsdam).

Gosh there's a lot to learn about being an inner-city trendy. Perhaps I'll stay where I am, wedged between the inner city's beard stubble and goatees and outer suburbia's comb-over's and mullets.

The rise of free and easy speeches

Speaking from the heart is such a modern thing to do

PERHAPS it's my time in life but I seem to be always at weddings and engagements and twenty-first birthdays these days. I love the speeches at these events. Unlike previous generations, twenty-somethings today seem to actually welcome the opportunity to talk openly, warmly and poignantly about their feelings and their emotions. This was simply not done a generation or two ago. Brides did not speak at weddings. Grooms stumbled their way through a few lines and then sat down to polite applause. Perhaps it's that the bride and groom today are more likely to be older—late, as opposed to early, twenties—and as such are more self-confident and especially in terms of speaking in front of elders.

Or is it that today's education system has encouraged young people to stand and pitch their ideas? Show and tell was not part of my primary schooling, although as a teaching technique it applied to my sister, just two years younger. Being part of the baby boomer cohort, my prep class in 1962 had forty-five kids; today's prep classes are half that. The same goes for family size: I was one of six kids; today's families are more likely to have two children. Big families and big class sizes are not conducive to bringing out the verbal skills of children. Back then, it was very much a case of children speaking when they were spoken to. And the same logic applies in parenting. If there are six children competing for parents' attention, less time can be allocated to each child.

And then there is the influence of modern pop and media culture, which seems to reward those who are best able to articulate and package their case. Television beams into our everyday lives the values and the verbal fluency of an increasingly globalised American culture. Generation Y insist on using the American *airplane* rather than the British *aeroplane*. They also pronounce *schedule* as 'sked-ule' and *Bernard* as 'Ber-Nard', both Americanisms. If generation Y have absorbed the pronunciations, why wouldn't they also absorb the American predilection for a classless society's unabashed self-confidence, combined with the kind of verbal fluency that is most likely to deliver commercial success?

In the 1960s Australia was still very much a stoic, British-based culture where children were expected to know their place. Knowing your place was part of a broader social milieu that constricted the notions of free thought and expression that are so apparent in young people today. Or at least that are so apparent to anyone aged fifty and over.

Indeed it is precisely this verbal self-confidence that so effortlessly bubbles forth at special events such as weddings, when twenty-somethings address wider demographic audiences. But it is not just the verbal fluency of this generation that strikes you; it is the content of their speeches. To hear loving, open and warm sentiment expressed by grooms to brides, by brides to grooms and by one friend to another in public and before family and friends is both humbling and confronting to older generations.

What social, educational and cultural transition—no, tsunami—took effect, and when, to produce such self-confident sentiment? Such sentiment, though eloquently packaged, can present to boomers and their elders as nothing less than public displays of being 'laid bare'. Such speeches would never have been made a generation ago for fear of some form of reprisal or ridicule, even from an audience of family and friends. That Australia fifty years ago was a hasher, narrower, crueller society than it is today is nowhere better evidenced than in the contrasting openness that generation Y display in their public orations to all and sundry about their experience with love and affection.

And finally ...

Can obsessions be decent?

OF COURSE obsessions can be decent. What's indecent about insisting on politeness and manners? What's indecent about going to bed early? Or managing personal finances efficiently? Or ensuring that there is a balance to small-talk situations? Or measuring the melon content in a fruit platter? Okay, so that last one is a little weird, but you get my point.

And it's not as if I am insisting that others do the same; what I am concerned about is not being subjected to the self-centred behaviour of others. Why should anyone continue a conversation with a person who turns everything that is said back into a story about them? And exactly what is wrong with having a penchant for punctuation? So what if I note those who can and can't spell The Philippines? Why should we sympathise with someone who bemoans the fact that they are continually broke when time after time they make silly life decisions?

Of course it's okay to obsess about behaviour, just so long as that obsession doesn't turn into prescription. I don't mind if you're a loud eater: just do your loud eating in a place where I am not forced to listen to it. Have some consideration! And I really don't mind if you stay out late going to a fashionable nightclub on a Thursday night. Just don't expect 'boring people' who don't do this sort of thing to carry your workload on a Friday morning 'because you've had a big night'. Why do some people feel entitled to special treatment and get indignant when they don't receive it?

The entitled generation isn't confined to generation Y; I think it also applies to baby boomers as well as to generation X. It seems to be a condition borne of the prosperity of the second half of the twentieth century. No

Great Depression. No world war. Here is a group of people born progressively from the 1950s onwards who, as they matured to adulthood, enjoyed a lifestyle that was immeasurably better than their parents.

It seems that such has been the rise in middle-class prosperity over decades that boomers now expect more from life as 'realistic' middle-aged parents than they ever did as 'idealistic' young adults. The shift to entitlement (and to self-centredness) might also be connected to the shrinking of the average family: there's simply more to go around when there's only two kids as opposed to six. And if mum goes back to work, or remains in the workforce, then there's even more to go around.

Why wouldn't the children of baby boomers and others get to thinking that 'the universe' always delivers: plasma televisions, mobile phones, branded clothing, cafés *for breakfast*, cheap overseas air travel and annual incomes that rise with age, expertise and application. This latter point wasn't always the case (say, around the 1930s) and indeed it's not the case today in some economically stagnant countries. That's why people have been so keen to emigrate from, say, Eastern Europe and more latterly from Ireland: effort isn't rewarded and opportunities are limited. This isn't the case in the New World and especially not in Australia.

Despite seasonal and even yearly ups and downs, over the longer term the quality of life in Australia has improved in line with increased prosperity, and this process seems to have engendered a growing communal sense of entitlement. If the world delivers such abundant opportunity, then over time we become more and more comfortable; with this comes self-interest and even narcissism. You will be fascinated with me and my life because, well, I am, so you must be too. Have a look at the Facebook or Twitter profiles of a random group of friends of all ages. There you'll find long dissertations about their favourite quotes, their favourite colours, their pets' names and, if you're lucky, the number of countries they've visited.

Hordes of people seem to be just waiting to be discovered for being, well, fabulous. Self-absorption was not an issue that afflicted Australians in the middle of the twentieth century and earlier. The thinking then was based around values and behaviours like sacrifice, frugality and austerity, as well as deference and hierarchy, though now the notion of 'doing your duty' sounds twee. There was no scope for individualism in the thinking of the frugal prewar generation. Any sign of it was met with: 'What? Do you think your special or somethin'?'

And so it is that by the early decades of the twenty-first century and more than sixty years after the end of World War II we see generations that are now centred more or less entirely on the notion of self. And if it isn't all about *my*self then it's all about *my* kids. That's why popular culture is so obsessed with baby boomers and their generation Y children. Xers only get a rare look in because they aren't boomers and they aren't boomers' kids. Have you noticed the way business (and government) is now inserting the word *you* and/or *my* into their products and websites? Clearly focus-group research shows that we connect better into a product when it is geared to and personalised to the individual. And that's because so many of us do think we're special.

This is not to say that the values and behaviours of the frugal generation were always ennobling: that generation was insensitive to, for example, matters relating to race and sex—although, to be fair, the people of one time should never be judged by the values of the people from another time. But the point is that society seems to have lost the notion of consideration for others. Indeed we seem to have lost what might otherwise be referred to as common courtesy.

This is a major theme of *Decent Obsessions*: it is the radical, heretical, perhaps even challenging idea that there is a individual responsibility to act civilly and, dare I say it, thoughtfully to others. It is the idea of putting others first! Yourself, second. I warned you it was radical. Do you think my idea will catch on? I have talked in this book about occasions where I have walked away from business functions marvelling at the rudeness of some people. I ask myself: 'Am I the only normal person on the planet?' Such was the response to a column I wrote on this subject that I set up a dedicated Facebook page for fellow 'normal' enthusiasts. The Facebook/Society for Normal People (SNP) now has 4000 followers.

But *Decent Obsessions* isn't just about the behaviour of others; it's also about the particulars of life and relationships. It might seem odd to obsess about the hygiene of sockless French men, but oddly enough this is the sort of thing that can occupy the mind, given the right circumstances. It is an acknowledgement of the brain's meanderings and the whimsical musings of daily life that fill the void between the important issues. Yes, there are big issues—national debt, refugees, structural change in employment—but what interests and engages most people most of the time has nothing to do with such matters. What interests most people most of the time is minutiae.

When I ran a column in *The Australian* about leaving the television volume on an even number as opposed to an odd number, I received an extraordinary response. It was as if people felt connected on an otherwise mundane matter: 'I feel that way too, but I've never said anything.' It's the realisation that we are all human, that we might all live independent lives, but that there's something that connects us. And that is the ordinariness of everyday life. It might be that everyone has a 'junk drawer' in the kitchen. It might be that they too have noted the pillowfication of the bedroom. It might be that they too are frustrated by drinks functions where the speeches don't start on time.

Life is full of frustrations and curiosities that connect us. This is what I mean by decent obsessions. There's nothing sinister about an obsession that is decent and in fact once brought out into the open, it can reassure, to their delight, that others think and feel exactly the same. I suspect that there are decent obsessions in all of us. It's just that we never thought they were worthy of discussion. Hopefully *Decent Obsessions* legitimises a broader discussion about the small stuff in life that counts.

Index